JANICE VANCLEAVE'S
Scientists Through the Ages

WILEY

John Wiley & Sons, Inc.

Published by John Wiley & Sons, Inc., Hoboken, New Jersey
Published simultaneously in Canada

Design and production by Navta Associates, Inc.

ISBN: 0-471-25222-0

Printed in the United States of America

10 9 8 7 6 5 4 3 2 1

Contents

Dedication

It is my pleasure to dedicate this book to two very knowledgeable and talented educators, Dixie Andersen and Marsha Willis. Dixie Andersen is the campus instructional coordinator (and librarian) for Navarro Academy in SAISD, San Antonio, Texas, and Marsha Willis is the middle school science coordinator at Region 12 Educational Center, Waco, Texas. Dixie's and Marsha's help in providing research information was invaluable. It is an honor to call these special educators my friends and colleagues.

My thanks to Dixie Andersen and Marsha Willis.

Acknowledgments

I wish to express my appreciation to these science specialists for their valuable assistance by providing information, assisting me in finding it, or both.

Members of the Central Texas Astronomical Society, including Johnny Barton, Dick Campbell, John W. McAnally, and Paul Derrick. Johnny is an officer of the club and has been an active amateur astronomer for more than twenty years. Dick is an amateur astronomer who is interested in science education. John is also on the staff of the Association of Lunar and Planetary Observers, where he is the acting assistant coordinator for transit timings of the Jupiter Section. Paul is the author of the "Stargazer" column in the *Waco Tribune-Herald.*

Dr. Glenn S. Orton, a senior research scientist at the Jet Propulsion Laboratory of California Institute of Technology, is an astronomer and a space scientist who specializes in investigating the structure and the composition of the planetary atmospheres. He is best known for his research on Jupiter and Saturn. I have enjoyed exchanging ideas with Glenn about astronomy facts and about modeling astronomy experiments.

Dr. Ben Doughty is the head of the physics department at Texas A & M University—Commerce, in Commerce, Texas. Ben has helped me to better understand the fun of learning about physics. Robert Fanick is a chemist at Southwest Research Institute in San Antonio, Texas, and Dr. Tineke Sexton is an instructor of biology and microbiology at Houston Community College Northwest in Houston, Texas.

A special note of gratitude to these educators who assisted by pretesting the activities, by providing scientific information, or both: Holly Harris, China Spring Middle School, China Spring, Texas; Anne Skrabanek, homeschooling consultant, Perry, Texas; Candi, Allie, and Nathaniel Stryker, homeschooling consultants; and Connie Chatmas, Sue Dunham, and Stella Cathey, consultants, Marlin, Texas.

Introduction

This book contains **biographical** (about a person's life) sketches of famous scientists from ancient to present times. It is divided into two parts: part I includes chapters about different types of scientists, and part II includes chapters about individual scientists, which are in alphabetical order by the scientists' last names.

In each chapter, you'll find interesting facts about the scientist, as well as a discovery experiment or an activity that will help you get to know the work of the scientist being presented. You can read the chapters and perform the experiments in any order.

Each chapter explains science terms in simple language that can be easily understood. New terms are boldfaced and defined the first time they are presented. The scientific concepts are explained in basic terms with little complexity and can be applied to many similar situations. With fun facts and experiments, this book will encourage you to learn through exploration and discovery.

HOW TO USE THIS BOOK

You can start at the beginning of the book, or you can just flip through the chapters for a scientist who sounds interesting. Before you do any of the experiments, read them through completely. Once you've decided on an experiment to try, collect all the needed materials and follow all procedures carefully. The format for each chapter is as follows:

- A brief biography of the scientist and information on his or her discoveries.

- **Fun Time!** A discovery investigation related to the scientist. Each experiment includes a **Purpose,** which states the objective of the investigation; a complete list of easy-to-find **Materials;** a step-by-step **Procedure;** a section identifying the expected **Results;** and a **Why?** section that explains why the experiment works.

- **More Fun with . . . !** An additional fun activity relating to the topic.

- **Book List** A list of other books about the scientist and the experiments.

GENERAL INSTRUCTIONS FOR THE EXPERIMENTS

1. Read the experiments completely before starting.

2. Collect the supplies. You will have less frustration and more fun if all the materials necessary for the activity are ready before you start. You lose your train of thought when you have to stop and search for supplies. Ask an adult for advice before substituting any materials.

3. Do not rush. Follow each step very carefully; never skip steps, and do not add your own. Safety is of the utmost importance, and

by reading each experiment before starting, then following the instructions exactly, you can feel confident that no unexpected results will occur.

4. Observe. If your results are not the same as those described in the experiment, carefully reread the instructions and start over from step 1.

I

TYPES OF SCIENTISTS

Astronomers

A **scientist** is someone who observes and/or experiments to discover answers. But a scientist doesn't necessarily need special training or have to be a certain age or sex. A scientist is anyone who searches for answers to scientific questions.

Celestial bodies are the natural objects in the sky, including suns, moons, planets, and stars. **Astronomy** is the study of celestial bodies in the **universe** (Earth and all celestial bodies in space regarded as a whole). There is no record of the first **astronomers** (scientists who study celestial bodies), but they were ancient peoples who looked at the heavens and tried to explain what they saw. These ancient astronomers studied the heavens without the aid of a **telescope** (an instrument that permits distant objects to be viewed as if they were brighter and closer to the observer). Their universe was what they saw around and above them. They studied the movements of the Sun, the Moon, the planets, and the stars and often used these changes to try to explain events on Earth.

To some ancient peoples, the universe was a mountain rising out of a sea with a dome over it. The dome was lighted by the Sun during the day and by the Moon and the stars at night. Stories such as this, which answer basic questions about the nature of the world or express the beliefs of a group of people, are called **myths.** Myths generally date before the introduction of writing and were passed orally from one generation to the next. The study of the myths of a particular culture is called **mythology.**

Astrology is a study that assumes that the positions and the motions of celestial bodies, particularly the Sun, the Moon, the planets, and the stars, at the time of a person's birth affect the person's character and therefore his or her destiny. Astrology is an ancient practice that seems to have developed independently in different civilizations. As early as 3000 B.C., the Chaldeans, who lived in Babylonia (now Iraq), studied astrology. Many scholars viewed astrology and astronomy as complementary sciences until about the 1500s. At that time, the discoveries made by such astronomers as the Polish priest and scientist Nicolaus Copernicus (1473–1543) and the Italian scientist Galileo Galilei (1564–1642) disproved some of the foundations of astrology. Since that time, scientists have considered astrology a **pseudoscience** (a set of beliefs pretending to be scientific but not based on scientific principles).

The branch of astronomy dealing with the study of the universe as a whole—its distant past and its future—is called **cosmology.** Many early scientists were Greek **philosophers,** which, as defined by the ancient Greeks, meant people who search for knowledge for its own sake. **Philosophy** (the investigation of truth, wisdom, and knowledge) included all areas of instruction, such as art, science, and religion. One famous Greek philosopher, Aristotle (384–322 B.C.), is thought to have been one of the earliest **cosmologists** (scientists who spe-

cialize in cosmology). Aristotle made many observations of the natural world and developed theories to explain things he saw. He was the most influential philosopher in the history of European thought for almost two 2,000 years. Even into the 1600s, Aristotle's theories were considered the truth by the Roman Catholic Church. To disagree with his ideas was considered **heresy** (an act against the teachings of a church, especially by a person professing the beliefs of that church) and was punishable by imprisonment or death. Galileo disagreed with Aristotle's theories on astronomy and narrowly escaped being killed.

One idea that Galileo disagreed with was Aristotle's **geocentric** (Earth-centered) theory of the universe, which put a stationary Earth at the center of the universe and had all the other heavenly bodies moving around it. Aristotle wasn't the first to express this idea. In fact, it had been the accepted theory for thousands of years. But since Aristotle agreed with it, it became the accepted theory for almost 2,000 more years. Another accepted idea that Galileo disagreed with was that all heavenly bodies, including the Moon, were perfectly smooth spheres.

Aristotle was a thinker, not an experimenter. He didn't try to prove his ideas. The Greek astronomer and mathematician Claudius Ptolemy, who lived in Alexandria (in Egypt) from approximately A.D. 100 to 170, created a model to explain the motion of celestial bodies in a geocentric universe. Since his model agreed with Aristotle's theory of the universe, its accuracy was basically unchallenged until Nicolaus Copernicus proposed a **heliocentric** (Sun-centered) model. There were so many unexplained parts to Copernicus's model that the Church didn't take it seriously, but many scientists of the day became interested, including the Danish astronomer Tycho Brahe (1546–1601) and the German astronomer Johannes Kepler (1571–1630). Brahe was at first reluctant to share his discoveries with others for fear they would take credit for his works. But in time Brahe and Kepler shared their ideas and research.

It wasn't easy for anyone to work with Brahe. Brahe once fought a duel with another man over who was the better mathematician. Brahe may have been the best mathematician, but his lack of skill at sword fighting resulted in his losing a part of his nose and having to wear a metal plate over it to hide the missing end.

Brahe and Kepler's combined efforts led to the discovery that planets must have an **elliptical** (the shape of a slightly flattened circle) **orbit** (the curved path of one object around another) around the Sun, not around Earth. Previously, it had been believed that the orbits were circular, not elliptical.

In 1609, Galileo started studying the sky with his own homemade telescopes. His observations provided proof of Copernicus's theory of a Sun-centered universe, but Galileo was forbidden by the Church to talk or write about his ideas. However, he had already published them, and other scientists were beginning to agree that the universe was heliocentric. The big missing piece to the puzzle was the force that kept celestial bodies in orbit. The English scientist Sir Isaac Newton (1642–1727) discovered this force, which is called **gravity** (the force of attraction between all objects in the universe). He worked out equations to explain how gravity affected the motion of celestial bodies. These equations were so accurate that they are still used today.

Newton thought that there were three basic parts of the universe: time, which was the same all over the universe; space, where every object had its own size and position; and **mass,** the amount of **matter** (the substance from which all objects are made) in an object, which was constant. Mass is commonly measured in metric units of grams and kilograms. In 1915, the German scientist Albert Einstein (1879–1955)

made waves in the astronomical community by disagreeing with Newton's theories. In his theory of relativity, Einstein showed that time, space, and mass were different for observers moving at different velocities in relation to one another. (A **theory** is an idea or a statement, based on evidence, that explains how or why something happens, but it can be changed as new information is discovered.)

The German-born British astronomers Caroline Herschel (1750–1848) and her brother William Herschel (1738–1822) made many important contributions to astronomy. Among these were eight comets, discovered by Caroline, and the planet Uranus, discovered by William. **Comets** are small celestial bodies made up of dust, gases, and ices (mainly, water and carbon dioxide) that move in an extremely elongated orbit around the Sun. Comets and planets are **natural satellites** (celestial bodies that revolve around other celestial bodies).

Caroline Herschel was the first acknowledged woman astronomer, but her accomplishments didn't cause any great changes in the attitude of the scientific community toward women scientists. Yet Caroline's scientific work, as well as that of other women scientists, such as the American astronomer Maria Mitchell (1818–1889), was a model for women scientists who followed. Mitchell was America's first, but certainly was not the last, recognized woman astronomer. Henrietta Leavitt's (1868–1921) astronomy studies made possible the first accurate determination of distances between celestial bodies.

Another modern astronomer is the famous English cosmologist Stephen Hawking (1942–). Hawking's most famous scientific contribution is providing better arguments for the presence of black holes in space. A **black hole** is thought to be an extremely dense celestial body that has such strong gravity that not even light can escape from it. Since light can enter it but cannot get out, it would appear to be black.

FUN TIME!

Purpose

To confirm Galileo's observations that the Moon is not a perfectly smooth sphere.

Materials

sheet of white copy paper
pen
ruler
binoculars and/or telescope

Procedure

1. Use the paper, pen, and ruler to draw a Moon Data table like the one below.

Moon Data	
Date	Diagram

2. Observe the Moon for as many days as possible during a 29-day period. During each observation, make a diagram of the Moon, shading in the dark areas.

3. Use the binoculars and/or a telescope to study the boundary on the Moon between the dark and the light parts. Make a note on your drawings about how straight or uneven this boundary is.

4. Label your drawings with the names of the different moon phases, as shown.

Results

Your observations should show that the boundary between the light and the dark sides of the Moon is uneven.

Why?

Using a telescope that he made, Galileo studied the **Moon phases** (regularly recurring changes in the shape of the lighted part of the Moon, facing Earth) and discovered that the boundary between the light and the dark sides of the Moon, called the **terminator,** was rough and uneven. From this and many other observations made with his telescope, Galileo concluded that the Moon's surface consists of valleys, plains, and mountains, much like the surface of Earth, so it is not perfectly smooth.

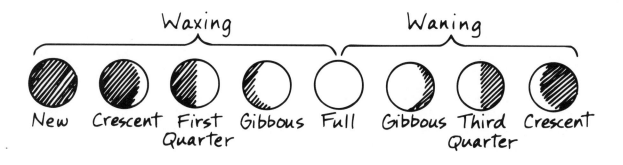

Waxing — Waning

New Crescent First Quarter Gibbous Full Gibbous Third Quarter Crescent

MORE FUN WITH THE MOON!

The same side of the Moon always faces Earth because the Moon **rotates** (turns about an **axis**—an imaginary line through the center of an object) and **revolves** (moves in an orbit— a curved path around an object) at the same rate. While the same lunar features are always seen by an observer on Earth, in the **Northern Hemisphere** (the region north of the **equator**—an imaginary line around the center of Earth) these features appear to rotate in a clockwise direction during the day. This is because an observer on Earth sees the Moon from a different direction as Earth rotates on its axis. The "Man in the Moon" (or, as seen by some, "The Moon Rabbit") is the design on the Moon that results from shadows made by its different land features. Make note of the position of the design when the Moon is in the eastern part of the sky and then again later when the Moon is in the western part of the sky. If the Moon is in a **crescent phase** (the lighted part of the Moon that looks like a ring segment with pointed ends), instead of observing its design, note any change in the direction that the pointed ends of the crescent face.

BOOK LIST

Filkin, David. *Stephen Hawking's Universe*. New York: BasicBooks, 1997. A brief history of the universe and the scientists who revealed its secrets.

Hathaway, Nancy. *The Friendly Guide to the Universe*. New York: Penguin Books, 1994. Information about the universe and the past and present scientists who have studied it.

VanCleave, Janice. *Astronomy for Every Kid*. New York: Wiley, 1991. Fun facts and investigations about celestial bodies and other astronomy topics.

2

Biologists

Biologists are scientists who specialize in **biology,** which is the study of **organisms** (living things). In 1800, the French **naturalist** (a scientist who studies plants and/or animals) Jean-Baptiste de Lamarck (1744–1829) introduced the word *biology.* Lamarck is also famous for developing a theory of inheritance, which attempted to explain how particular **traits** (characteristics) are passed down from parents to their **offspring** (the young of a particular organism). Lamarck's scientific theory of

inheritance and his other theories were largely ignored or attacked during his lifetime, and he spent most of his days struggling to make a living. He was so poor that he was buried in a rented grave; after five years his body was removed, and no one knows where his remains are now.

A scientist who studies **microbes** (tiny organisms visible only under a microscope) is called a **microbiologist.** The founder of **microbiology** (the study of microbes) was

Antoni van Leeuwenhoek (1632–1723), who prepared his own microscopes and studied everything from blood to scrapings from his teeth. In 1865, the French scientist Louis Pasteur (1822–1895) published his findings that some microbes cause diseases. Pasteur called these disease-causing microbes **germs.** A later microbiologist who was able to discover a cure for diseases caused by microbes was Alexander Fleming (1881–1955).

One of the earliest detailed studies of organisms was made by the British naturalist Charles Darwin (1809–1882). His renowned studies were made aboard the HMS *Beagle,* during a British science expedition that traveled around the world from 1831 to 1836. Darwin studied plants and animals everywhere he went. From his studies, he proposed the **theory of natural selection,** sometimes called "survival of the fittest." This theory is based on the fact that all living organisms compete for things like water, food, and shelter, in order to survive Those organisms with traits best suited for survival live and produce offspring with traits similar to their own. For example, in areas where trees are tall, giraffes with longer necks would compete for food more successfully and would live to produce offspring with long necks like themselves. **Genetics** is the branch of biology that deals with the study of **heredity,** which is the transfer of traits (characteristics) from parents to offspring. **Geneticists** are scientists who study things that deal with heredity.

In the 1900s, the Austrian monk Gregor Johann Mendel (1822–1884) made the greatest single contribution to the study of heredity. Most scientists of that time supported the "blending" theory of heredity, which basically said that hereditary material from both parents blends together in the offspring. Mendel experimentally disproved the blending theory by using plants. He agreed with earlier scientists who said that separate units were passed from parents to offspring, and he guessed correctly that some of the units were **dominant** (this refers to the stronger of a pair of traits; when present, this determines the trait of the offspring). Other units were **recessive** (this refers to the weaker of a pair of traits; this doesn't determine the trait of an offspring if a dominant unit is present). The units of heredity described by Mendel were named **genes.**

It was not until the 1920s that the chemical structure of genetic material was determined to be made of proteins and a substance called deoxyribonucleic acid, or DNA. **Proteins** are chemicals in the body that are used in almost everything cells do. In 1953, the British biologist Francis Crick (1916–) and the American biologist James Watson (1928–) determined the structure of DNA. Some people report that these scientists were assisted by information collected by the American biologist Rosalind Franklin (1920–1958). Franklin died before a Nobel Prize was presented in 1962 to Watson and Crick for their DNA work. Rosalind Franklin was not mentioned as being a contributor.

While some scientists were searching for the makeup of genes, the American geneticist Barbara McClintock (1902–1992) investigated the effect of the location of genes. McClintock started her research because she became curious about the arrangements of the colored kernels in Indian corn. For years she studied the genes of corn and in 1952 concluded that the positions of genes on a **chromosome** (a rod-shaped structure in cells that is made up of genes) are not fixed; instead, the genes sometimes move or "jump" around unpredictably. It took about 25 years for the value of her work to be recognized. In 1983, she was the first woman to receive a Nobel Prize in medicine for work she did alone.

The American molecular biologist and Nobel Prize–winner Paul Berg (1926–) was the first scientist to combine DNA molecules from two different organisms. This combination made possible a whole new industry called **genetic engineering** (the application of the knowledge obtained from genetic investigations). Genetic engineering is used to change the traits of organisms. This allows genetic engineers to produce special kinds of plants or animals that can survive in certain environments. Today, biologists are investigating **cloning** (the process of producing an organism from one cell of a single parent). A cloned organism is genetically identical to its parent.

Botany, the branch of biology dealing with the study of plants, was founded around 330 B.C. by the Greek philosopher Theophrastus (c.372–c.287 B.C.), who was a student of Aristotle's. Biologists who specialize in plants, such as the Canadian-born Alice Eastwood (1859–1953), are called **botanists.** Starting in 1892, Eastwood worked at the California Academy of Science in San Francisco. After the earthquake of 1906, which destroyed the academy's plant collection, she spent years traveling and collecting plants. She inspired other women to become botanists, including the Mexican American Ynes Mexia (1870–1938). In 1933, Eastwood, at 74, and Mexia, then 63, traveled to Mexico to collect plants. In all, Eastwood collected more than 250,000 specimens for the academy. Mexia, who did not start her career as a botanist until she was 55, was able to collect about 150,000 specimens.

Other biologists, such as the British naturalist Jane Goodall (1934–), study animals. These scientists are called **zoologists. Zoology** (the branch of biology dealing with the study of animals) was founded around 350 B.C. by Aristotle. Fascinated as a child by the stories of Tarzan, Goodall dreamed of living in the jungles of Africa with wild animals, just as Tarzan did. Her dream came true, but even more than this, she became world renowned for her studies of chimpanzees.

The study of the relationship between plants and animals and their **environment** (all external factors affecting an organism, including **abiotic** [nonliving] and **biotic** [living] factors) is called **ecology.** Scientists who study this relationship between organisms and where they live, like Rachel Carson (1907–1964), are called **ecologists** (scientists who study living things and their environments). Carson was also a writer, and her book *Silent Spring* led to the ban on the **pesticide** (chemicals used to kill unwanted organisms, such as insects) called DDT.

FUN TIME!

Purpose

To model "jumping" genes.

Materials

10 colored beads: 2 black, 2 red, 2 white, 2 green, 2 yellow (2 beads of other colors may be substituted)

2 round toothpicks

a grape-size piece of clay

Procedure

1. Using one of each color, thread five beads on one of the toothpicks in this order: black, red, white, green, yellow.

2. Break the clay into four pieces. Stick two pieces on either end of the toothpick with the beads.

3. String the remaining beads on the second toothpick in this order: black, white, red, green, yellow.

4. Stick the remaining clay pieces on the ends of that toothpick.

5. Lay the beaded toothpicks side by side, with the black beads to the left, and compare the arrangement of beads on each toothpick.

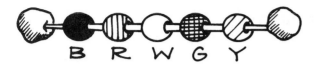

B R W G Y

B W R G Y

sage. Use beads of different colors, letting the different colors represent a letter of the alphabet, as shown. Prepare a key that explains which colors equal which letters. Then string the beads in a specific order so that they spell out a name or a message. You may wish to give the necklace and the key to a friend.

Results

The order of the colors of the second and third beads on the toothpicks is reversed.

Why?

The beaded toothpicks represent chromosomes, and the beads are genes. New cells are made by cell division (a cell splits into two new cells). In order for the two cells formed from one cell to have the same number and kind of chromosomes, each chromosome makes a copy of itself before the cell divides. Sometimes the copy is not exactly like the original. The order of the genes is like a coded message. When the order of the genes is changed, the message is different. Barbara McClintock called genes that were not in their normal sequence "jumping genes." Her research on jumping genes helped explain how normal cells can change into cancerous cells.

MORE FUN WITH GENES!

The genes on a chromosome are like letters of the alphabet. When the genes are arranged in a specific sequence, they form the message describing a specific protein. Make a chromosome necklace that spells out a secret mes-

BOOK LIST

Bernstein, Leonard. *Latino Women of Science.* Maywood, N. J.: People Publishing Co., 1998. Biographies about women scientists, including Ynes Mexia.

Goodall, Jane. *My Life with the Chimpanzees.* New York: Pocket Books, 1996. The fascinating story of one of the world's most celebrated naturalists, Jane Goodall.

Gribbin, John. *A Brief History of Science.* New York: Barnes & Noble, 1998. Information about different branches of science, including genetics, and how these developed.

VanCleave, Janice. *Animals.* New York: Wiley, 1992. Experiments about animals. Each chapter contains ideas that can be turned into award-winning science fair projects.

———. *The Human Body for Every Kid.* New York: Wiley, 1995. Facts and fun, simple experiments about the human body.

3

Chemists

A **chemical** is any substance with a definite composition made up of one or more **elements** (basic chemical substances of which all things are made; substances that contain only one kind of atom and that cannot be broken down into simpler substances). A **chemist** is a scientist who specializes in **chemistry,** which is the study of the makeup, the structure, of chemicals, as well as of how they change and combine. A chemical change is called a **chemical reaction** (a process by which atoms interact to form one or more new substances). Substances that are changed during a chemical reaction are called **reactants,** and substances produced in a chemical reaction are called **products.**

The first deliberate use of chemistry by ancient people may have been **fermentation** (a chemical reaction in which microbes growing in the absence of air cause changes in food).

We know that the Egyptians used the fermentation of fruit juices and grains to produce wine by around 1800 B.C.

In 580 B.C., the Greek philosopher Thales (625?–?546 B.C.) introduced the idea of elements, and around 440 B.C., the Greek philosopher Leucippus (450–370 B.C.) suggested that all matter was made of tiny, indivisible parts. Later, his pupil Democritus (c.460–c.370 B.C.) further developed the idea and called these parts **atoms.** Around 350 B.C., Aristotle taught that all matter was composed of four elements: earth, water, air, and fire. According to his theory, materials in nature were different from one another because they contained different amounts of these four elements. Therefore, changing the ratio of the elements in a substance could transform it into another substance. This theory laid the foundation for a study called **alchemy** (a mixture of science and magic that dealt with changing less-expensive metals into gold and with finding ways to prolong life indefinitely). The **alchemists** (scientists who practiced alchemy) were at one time well respected and were often supported by rulers who hoped that the alchemists would make gold for them. Some alchemists were frauds, but even those who believed in their work never succeeded in making gold or eternal life elixirs. In the seventeenth century, several new discoveries discredited alchemy, and it dwindled steadily in importance. By the eighteenth century, alchemy had been replaced by the study that we today call modern chemistry.

In 1651 an English chemist, Robert Boyle (1627–1691), defined elements as substances that are incapable of being simplified; this became the basis of modern chemistry. He is best remembered for Boyle's law, a physical law that explains how the pressure and the volume of a gas are related.

In the late seventeenth century, the German chemists Johann Becher (1635–1682) and Georg Stahl (1660–1734) both contributed to the **phlogiston theory,** which described burning as the result of the presence of **phlogiston** (an invisible, weightless substance in materials that can burn). According to their phlogiston theory, every substance capable of burning contained phlogiston, and during burning, the substance lost its phlogiston. Later, the British chemist Joseph Priestley (1733–1804) discovered that a gas he called "new air" caused candles to burn brightly. The French chemist Antoine-Laurent Lavoisier's (1743–1794) investigations disproved the phlogiston theory and showed that the "new air," which he called oxygen, was necessary for burning.

In 1846, the French chemist Louis Pasteur discovered that microbes in wine caused it to sour. In 1865, Pasteur devised a process to inhibit the souring of wine and milk by heating, which destroys harmful microbes. This process is named **pasteurization** after Pasteur.

In 1866, the Swedish chemist Alfred Bernhard Nobel (1833–1896) invented dynamite. He later regretted it because people were using his invention in wars, so he came up with a way to help promote peace, as well as science achievements, in the world. In his will, Nobel specified that most of his fortune be used to fund one prize each year in the fields of chemistry, economics, literature, physics, and physiology or medicine, as well as one for the promotion of world peace. The coveted award is called the Nobel Prize, and the first prizes were given in 1901. The Dutch chemist Jacobus H. van't Hoff (1852–1911) received the first prize in chemistry. In 1903, the Swedish chemist Svante August Arrhenius (1859–1927) received the Nobel Prize in chemistry for identifying electrically charged particles called **ions** (atoms or a group of atoms that has lost or gained one or more electrons). According to Arrhenius, substances, such as acids and bases, break apart and form ions in an **aqueous solution** (a mixture in which one or more substances are dissolved in water). Acids are substances that contain hydrogen and yield hydrogen ions (H^+) in an aqueous solution. Today, an **acid** is defined as an aqueous solution containing **hydronium ions**—H_3O^+, which are produced by the combination of a hydrogen ion (H^+) from the acid and a molecule of water (H_2O). Arrhenius's description of bases is the same as is used today, which is that a **base** is an aqueous solution containing **hydroxide ions**—OH^-. Identifying ions was a key to understanding chemical reactions.

In 1908, the British scientist Ernest Rutherford (1871–1937) received a Nobel Prize in chemistry for his investigations of **radioactive elements** (elements in which the nucleus breaks apart, giving off particles and energy). These investigations led to his discovery that atoms have a **nucleus** (the central part) containing **protons** (positively charged particles). Rutherford described an atom as consisting largely of empty space, with electrically positive charges in the nucleus in the center and **electrons** (electrically negative particles) orbiting the nucleus.

A **biochemist** is a scientist who specializes in **biochemistry,** which is the study of the **biochemicals** (substances found in organisms), including **organic chemicals** (substances containing the element **carbon**) and of the chemical reactions of life processes. In 1964, the British biochemist Dorothy Crowfoot Hodgkin (1910–1994) received a Nobel Prize in chemistry for her work in discovering the structure of two biochemical compounds, penicillin and vitamin B-12. Penicillin is used to kill infections in the body, and vitamins are necessary for body functions. By knowing the structure of these chemicals, scientists are able to make **synthetic** (man-made, not natural) penicillin and vitamin B-12.

FUN TIME!

Purpose

To determine the effect of acids and bases on a red cabbage indicator.

Materials

pen
masking tape
three 10-ounce (300-mL) clear plastic cups
tablespoon (15 mL) measuring spoon
white vinegar, 5%
distilled water
½ teaspoon (2.5 mL) baking soda
sheet of white copy paper
red cabbage indicator (see Appendix)
3 stirring spoons

Procedure

1. Use the pen and the tape to label the cups "Acid," "Base," and "Neutral."

2. Add 1 tablespoon (15 mL) of vinegar to the "Acid" cup, 1 tablespoon (15 mL) of distilled water and ½ teaspoon (2.5 mL) of baking soda to the "Base" cup, and 1 tablespoon (15 mL) of distilled water to the "Neutral" cup. Note: Wash the spoon in distilled water after each use so that you do not contaminate the contents of the different cups.

3. Set the cups on the sheet of white paper so that it will be easier for you to detect color changes.

4. Add 1 tablespoon (15 mL) of indicator to each cup. Using different spoons, stir the contents of each cup. Observe the color of the contents of each cup.

Results

The red cabbage indicator turns red in vinegar, remains purple in water, and turns blue to blue green in baking soda.

Why?

Chemicals are combinations of elements. Each element is made of building blocks called atoms, and the same kind of atoms makes up each specific element. Indicators are natural or synthetic chemical substances that change color in response to other chemicals. Acid/base indicators change colors in the presence of an **acid** (a substance that makes the red cabbage indicator turn from purple to red) or a **base** (a substance that makes the red cabbage indicator turn from purple to green).

Red cabbage contains a chemical that is one of a class of compounds called anthocyanins. The anthocyanin pigment in red cabbage is an acid/base indicator. Vinegar is known to be an acid, and baking soda is a base.

MORE FUN WITH ACIDS!

You can make eggshells dance! Peel off the shell from a boiled egg, and discard the contents or save the egg to eat later. Break the eggshell into small pieces, and place them into a jar of vinegar. The vinegar chemically reacts with the calcium carbonate in the shell and produces carbon dioxide gas. The bubbles of carbon dioxide stick to the shell pieces and act like little life preservers, causing the shells to float. As the shells rise, some of the bubbles get knocked away and the shells sink again. When more bubbles are made, the pieces float again. The shells will rise and sink in the vinegar until all of the calcium carbonate is used up and they disappear.

BOOK LIST

VanCleave, Janice. *Chemistry for Every Kid.* New York: Wiley, 1989. Fun, simple chemistry experiments, including information about acids.

———. *Molecules.* New York: Wiley, 1993. Experiments with acids and various types of molecules. Each chapter contains ideas that can be turned into award-winning science fair projects.

Wood, Robert. *Science for Kids: 39 Easy Chemistry Experiments.* Blue Ridge Summit, Pa.: TAB Books, 1991. Experiments that examine the makeup of substances and the changes that take place in them.

Yount, Lisa. *Antoine Lavoisier: Founder of Modern Chemistry.* Berkeley Heights, N.J.: Enslow, 2001. A biography of Lavoisier, the founder of modern chemistry.

4

Earth Scientists

Earth science is the study of Earth from the outermost limits of its **atmosphere** (a blanket of gas surrounding a celestial body) to the innermost depths of its interior. Earth science includes these fields of study: geology, meteorology, paleontology, and oceanography.

    Geology is the study of the composition of Earth and its history. Although geology originated as a modern scientific study in the eighteenth century, people have been collecting knowledge about Earth from ancient times. Prehistoric man had to make comparisons of the best stones to use for tools. By the early nineteenth century, many people were studying geological topics, but the term **geologist** (a scientist who studies things dealing with the composition of Earth and its history) was not yet in general use. Scientists, such as the Scottish geologist Charles Lyell (1797–1875), wanted to establish geology as a scientific field, like chemistry or physics. Lyell's writings greatly influenced the development of modern geology. In 1912, the German geologist Alfred Wegener (1880–1930) proposed the idea that the continents were once connected but in time drifted apart, which is called the **theory of continental drift.** Scientists of the early twentieth century found evidence to back up the theory of continental drift.

Meteorology is the study of Earth's atmosphere and especially the study of **weather** (the condition of the atmosphere at a certain time and place). A **meteorologist** is a scientist who specializes in meteorology. About 340 B.C., the Greek philosopher Aristotle wrote *Meteorologica,* which summed up the knowledge at that time about natural science, including weather and climate. The term *meteorology* comes from the Greek word *meteoros,* meaning "high in the sky," which was used for anything that fell from the sky (including rain and snow) and anything that was in the sky (including clouds). Theophrastus, a pupil of Aristotle's, later wrote a book about weather **forecasting** (predicting a future event), called the *Book of Signs.* His work consisted of ways to foretell the weather by noticing various weather-related indicators, such as a red sky in the morning, which is often followed by rain. Aristotle's and Theophrastus's work has influenced the study of weather and weather forecasting for nearly 2,000 years.

Meteorology did not become a genuine science until the invention of weather instruments, such as the **thermometer** (an instrument used to measure **temperature**—how hot or cold something is) and the **barometer** (an instrument used to measure **atmospheric pressure**—the force that gases in the atmosphere exert on a particular area). Galileo invented a crude thermometer in the late 1500s. The Italian mathematician and scientist Evangelista Torricelli (1608–1647), a student of Galileo's, invented the barometer in 1643. Torricelli thought that there must be a column of **air** (the name given to the mixture of gases in Earth's atmosphere) above a person, which would result in thousands of pounds (kg) of air continuously pushing on the person's body. Torricelli died before he was able to test and prove his hypothesis. The French mathematician and scientist Blaise Pascal (1623–1662) tested Torricelli's theory by having different people set up barometers at different places along a mountain slope. At the bottom of the mountain, the height of the mercury in the barometers was lower than at the top of the mountain, indicating a greater pressure at the bottom of the mountain. These results confirmed Torricilli's hypothesis that more air above the barometer at the lower **altitude** (the height of an object above Earth's surface, or **sea level**—the height of ocean water) would push down more on the mercury, causing the mercury to be lower in the barometer.

In 1667, Robert Hooke (1635–1703), an English scientist, invented the **anemometer** (an instrument used to measure wind speed). The German scientist Gabriel Daniel Fahrenheit (1686–1736) introduced the alcohol thermometer in 1709 and the mercury thermometer in 1714. In 1724, he introduced a temperature scale, which is named after him, the Fahrenheit scale. The Swedish astronomer Anders Celsius (1701–1744) devised the Celsius thermometer scale, which originally had 0° as the boiling point of water and 100° as water's freezing point. This scale was soon reversed, so that 0° was water's freezing point and 100° was water's boiling point; this scale is used today. In 1780, Horace de Saussure (1740–1799), a Swiss geologist and meteorologist, invented the hair **hygrometer** (an instrument used to measure **humidity**—the amount of water in air). The hair shortened as it dried and lengthened when wet, thus moving the pointer to which it is attached.

The science of meteorology benefited from advances in other sciences. For example, in 1752, the American statesman, amateur scientist, and inventor Benjamin Franklin (1706–1790) demonstrated the electrical nature of lightning by flying a kite in a thunderstorm. The first system of classifying and naming clouds was created by Luke Howard (1772–1864) in 1803. In 1806, the British admiral and **hydrographer** (a scientist who measures, describes, and maps the Earth's surface waters) Francis Beaufort (1774–1857) designed a wind scale to indicate wind speeds. The **telegraph** (a device used to send and receive a code of electrical signals), which was invented in 1843 by the American inventor Samuel Morse (1791–1872), allowed meteorologists from different areas to share information. Thus weather could be better forecast. Today, **artificial satellites** (objects purposely placed into orbit around Earth, other planets, or the Sun) allow meteorologists to know the weather conditions across the world. Tiros 1, the first weather satellite, was launched in 1960.

Paleontology is the study of prehistoric animal and plant life through the careful examination of **fossils** (remains or traces of prehistoric plants and animals). **Paleontologists** are scientific observers of fossils. The collection and study of fossils began in the late seventeenth century when the English scientist Robert Hooke examined the fossils of marine creatures. The British scientist Mary Anning (1799–1847) is one of the first recognized women paleontologists. The field of paleontology grew as more fossils were discovered around the world. Modern paleontologists have used the fossil record to divide Earth's history into periods, based on the kinds of life that were present.

Oceanography is the study of oceans, including the organisms in them. **Oceanographers** are scientists who specialize in oceanography. Written records of significant biological observations concerning marine organisms began with Aristotle. For about 2,000 years, it was generally accepted that Aristotle had already discovered and described everything there was to know about science, as well as about other topics. Around the sixteenth century, amateur naturalists started making studies of the ocean. Many of these were explorers; notable are the explorations of the German naturalist and explorer Alexander von Humboldt (1769–1859) and the British explorer James Cook (1728–1779), who made extensive voyages and observations of the oceans. Even Benjamin Franklin studied the ocean. Franklin was interested in many things, and he made some of the earliest studies of convection currents in the ocean.

Ocean convection currents are the movement of water in a circular pattern as lighter, warm water rises and heavier, cool water sinks. Franklin studied the convection currents in the Atlantic Ocean, known as the Gulf Stream, which is a surface current off the eastern coast of North America. Franklin found that this current was warmer than the water around it and that the warm water stayed together, so that there was a sharp boundary between the warm current and the cold water surrounding it.

Interest in oceanographic and marine biological studies increased during the nineteenth century. Charles Darwin made significant contributions to marine biology, as a result of working aboard the English ship HMS *Beagle* as a naturalist on a science expedition that went around the world (1831–1836). In 1855, Matthew Maury (1806–1873), who is known as the father of U.S. oceanography, published *The Physical Geography of the Seas*. This book contained sailing records of ships that Maury used to chart the ocean's currents.

In the past, scientists examined underwater ocean material by collecting whatever they could in containers dropped into the water. A portable breathing device for divers, called the **SCUBA** (Self-Contained Underwater Breathing Apparatus), invented in 1939 for the U.S. military, allowed scientists to descend into the water to make observations, as well as to collect materials and take pictures. In 1977, the first manned **submersible** (a sea craft that can function underwater at great depths), called **Alvin,** was used to visit the wreckage of the famous ship the *Titanic*. Alvin and other manned submersibles have allowed observations of a marine environment previously not seen because of the ocean's extreme depth. Even so, there is much less knowledge of the marine world than of the **terrestrial** (land) environment.

FUN TIME!

Purpose

To determine how temperature affects the movement of water.

Materials

two 10-ounce (300-mL) transparent plastic
   cups
cold and warm tap water
blue food coloring
spoon
ice tray
freezer

Procedure

1. Fill one of the cups with cold water.

2. Add 10 or more drops of food coloring to make the water a deep blue. Stir with the spoon.

3. Pour the colored water into the ice tray, and place the tray in a freezer until the water is frozen. This can take 2 or more hours.

4. Fill the remaining plastic cup three-fourths full with warm water.

5. Remove the ice tray from the freezer and take out one colored ice cube. Return the tray to the freezer until needed for the following "More Fun with Currents" activity.

6. Place the ice cube in the cup of water.

7. Observe the water in the cup near and below the ice cube.

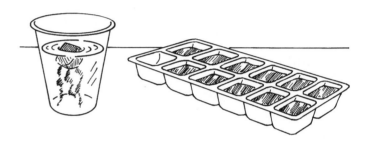

Results

Streams of blue move downward from the ice cube.

Why?

The warm water in the cup melts the ice, and the colder, colored water sinks. The cold water sinks because the density of cold water is greater than the density of warm water. **Density** is the measure of the amount of matter in a known volume of a material. Density can be used to compare the heaviness of materials. The greater the density, the heavier the material. Cold water has a greater density than does warm water, so cold water will sink in warm water. The movement of water due to differences in temperature produces **convection currents.**

MORE FUN WITH CURRENTS!

If all the materials used are clean, you can create a drinkable green lemonade. Fill a drinking glass with the blue ice cubes. Add yellow lemonade to the glass. As the ice melts and the blue-colored water mixes with the yellow lemonade, a green liquid will be produced. You can experiment with different colored liquids and different colored ice cubes.

BOOK LIST

Allaby, Michael. *How the Weather Works.* Pleasantville, N.Y.: Reader's Digest Association, 1995. Outlines the history of meteorology and provides weather experiments.

Oliver, Ray. *Rocks & Fossils.* New York: Random House, 1993. Information about rocks and fossils and step-by-step procedures for identifying and displaying them.

VanCleave, Janice. *Earth Science for Every Kid.* New York: Wiley, 1991. Fun facts and investigations about earth science.

———. *Oceans for Every Kid.* New York: Wiley, 1996. Fun facts and investigations about oceans, including currents.

Wood, Robert. *Science for Kids: 39 Easy Geology Experiments.* Blue Ridge Summit, Pa.: TAB Books, 1991. Experiments that examine the physical nature of Earth.

5

Physicists

Physicists are scientists who study physics. **Physics** is the study of the properties and the relationships of matter and **energy** (the capacity to move matter from one place to another) and the motion of matter. Energy is the ability to do **work,** which is the amount of **force** (the push or pull on an object's matter) on an object times the distance the object moves in the direction of the force.

Matter is anything that takes up space and has mass. Matter describes all of the physical substances around us: your body, food you eat, clothes you wear, and so on. Around 400 B.C., the Greek philosopher Democritus developed the idea suggested by his teacher Leucippus that all matter was made of atoms. Democritus thought that the physical properties of matter were due to the shape of atoms and whether or not they hooked together. Aristotle said that Democritus's ideas about atoms were wrong and that matter was a combination of four things: earth, fire, air, and water.

The Greek physicist Archimedes (287–212 B.C.) wasn't as concerned with the makeup of matter as he was with its physical properties. He figured out a way to measure an object's **volume** (the amount of space taken up by an object), and he discovered that different materials, such as gold and silver, had different densities (the comparison of the mass of an object to its volume).

Aristotle's ideas about atoms were basically accepted until the early 1800s, when the British scientist John Dalton (1766–1844) gave his opinion about atoms. Based on his experiments and observations, Dalton suggested that all atoms of one element were the same and were different from atoms of another element. He also thought that atoms could not be broken into smaller parts. By the early 1900s, it had been discovered experimentally that atoms were made of smaller particles: uncharged particles **(neutrons)** and positive particles (protons) in the nucleus (the central part), with negative particles (electrons) spinning around the nucleus.

Electricity is a form of energy associated with the presence and the movement of electrical charges. An **electrical charge** is the property of particles within atoms that causes the particles to attract or repel one another or other materials. Around 600 B.C., the Greek philosopher Thales is believed to have been the first to experimentally discover the effect of electrical charges. Thales rubbed **amber** (fossilized tree sap) on cat fur and found that it would pick up bits of straw and feathers. The first scientific study of electricity was made in the 1600s by the physician William Gilbert (1544–1603). He was the first to use the term *electric* to describe the force that substances exert after being rubbed. Thales and Gilbert experimented with what is now known as **static charges,** which is the build-up of stationary electrical charges.

Electrical charges occur in nature in two forms. In 1747, before atoms and atomic particles were discovered, the American scientist Benjamin Franklin experimented with **static electricity** (any effect due to static charges) and named the two charges positive and negative. In 1752, Franklin performed his famous experiment, in which he flew a kite during a thunderstorm. Franklin's kite experiment was done to prove that lightning and electricity were the same thing.

In 1800, Alessandro Volta (1745–1827), the Italian physicist known for his pioneering work in electricity, invented the first **battery** (a device that changes chemical energy into electrical energy). The ability to harness electricity led to many electrical inventions. On March 10, 1876, the American scientist Alexander Graham Bell (1847–1922) invented the **telephone** (an instrument that changes sound into electrical messages and back again). Another famous scientist who worked with electricity was Thomas Alva Edison (1847–1931); among his many inventions was a practical electric lightbulb. Countless electrical devices have been developed since then, including computers.

At the end of the eighteenth century, another form of energy, heat, was described by the French chemist Antoine Lavoisier as the transfer of **caloric,** which was believed to be an invisible, weightless substance inside materials that flowed from a hot object to a cold object when the two objects were in contact. A short time after Lavoisier's death, the American physicist Sir Benjamin Thompson (1753–1814), later known as Count Rumford, proved the caloric theory to be incorrect. He was one of the first to show that work could be converted to heat. Even so, the caloric theory continued to be accepted by most scientists.

In 1799, the British chemist Sir Humphry Davy (1778–1829) suggested that hot objects do not contain heat. Instead, hot objects may give up heat and cold objects absorb heat, but they don't contain heat. Between 1840 and 1849, the British physicist James Prescott Joule (1818–1889) provided further experimental evidence that this is true. Thus **heat** is the energy transferred from one body to another, due to differences in temperature. The internal energy of the body before or after a heat transfer is called its **thermal energy** (internal energy that affects the temperature of an object).

Energy that is released as a result of splitting or fusing atomic nuclei is called **nuclear energy.** The French physicist Pierre Curie (1859–1906) and the Polish physicist Marie Curie (1867–1934) studied the nuclear energy given off when a change occurs in the nucleus of an atom, which Marie called **radioactivity.** Marie also coined the term **radioactive,** which describes the ability of an element to **spontaneously** (happening by itself) give off what is now known as **particle radiation** (particles given off from the nucleus of some elements). In the 1950s, with the American physician Solomon Aaron Berson (1918–1972), the American physicist Rosalyn Sussman Yalow (1921–) developed a medical procedure for using radioactive elements to identify physical problems in the body.

Physicists have long been fascinated by matter in motion. Aristotle erroneously taught that heavy objects fall faster than lighter objects. About 2,000 years later, Galileo proved Aristotle wrong by doing an experiment. Galileo placed a lightweight object on top of a heavier one and dropped them. They fell together. Galileo's conclusion was that air slowed lightweight objects, but heavier ones could push through it. Galileo thought that without air, all objects would fall at the same rate. He did not have the necessary tools to test his idea, but in 1650, the German

physicist Otto von Guericke (1602–1686) invented the air pump, which could take all the air out of a chamber. Galileo was proven to be right. All objects fell at the same rate in the airless chamber.

Neither Aristotle nor Galileo identified the reason that things fall. That was done later by the English physicist Sir Isaac Newton, who identified the force as gravity. Newton introduced the idea that gravity not only pulls things toward Earth but also keeps the planets in orbit.

Another claim of the ancient Greek philosophers was that to keep an object moving, a constant force must be applied. But the Islamic scientist Alhazen (965–1039) was the first to propose that a moving object moves endlessly unless a force stops it or changes its direction of motion. Even so, the Greek view was more accepted. Later, Galileo agreed with Alhazen, and still later, Newton described this physical law as **inertia** (the property of matter that causes it to resist any change in motion). Inertia is the first of three famous laws of motion developed by Newton, which describe the motions of objects and their response to forces.

Galileo is credited as being the first to suggest **relative motion** (the description of motion from a specific frame of reference). For example, if you are in a moving car, all the objects in the car don't appear to be moving, but if you look outside the window, you would see a building moving by. In other words, to describe motion, you have to have something, a frame of reference, to compare the motion to. If the objects in the car are your frame of reference, you are not moving in comparison to them. But if the buildings outside the car are your frame of reference, you are moving in comparison to them. In 1915, Albert Einstein's theory of relativity showed that it would take more energy than is contained in the universe for something with mass to travel at the speed of light, which is 186,000 miles per second (300,000 km/sec). But if objects could travel near the speed of light, they would age more slowly as viewed by an observer not traveling at this speed. This means that if one twin left Earth in a rocket ship traveling near light speed, when he returned, he would be younger than his twin brother. Though humans have yet to travel at such a speed, some radioactive particles that naturally **decay** (a spontaneous change of the nucleus of one radioactive element into another) have been accelerated to fast-enough speeds to slow down their aging process, which means that they decay more slowly.

FUN TIME!

Purpose

To demonstrate the apparent difference in the motion of an object.

Materials

rotating chair
book

Procedure

1. Sit in the chair and hold the book at an angle, with its bottom against your chest.

2. Push on the floor with your feet so that the chair turns toward your right.

3. Look at the bottom edge of the book and determine any motion of the book relative to your chest. In other words, does the book appear to move while your chest remains stationary?

4. Repeat steps 1 and 2 while looking at the top edge of the book. Determine any motion of the book relative to the objects in the room.

Results

The book does not appear to move when compare to your chest, but it appears to move toward your right when compared to the objects in the room.

Why?

Relative motion is the description of motion from a specific frame of reference. When you were turning around, the book did not appear to move when your chest was the frame of reference. This is because your chest and the book were both moving together. Thus, when you compared the motion of the book to an object moving at the same speed as the book, the book appeared not to be moving. But when the objects in the room were the frame of reference, the objects were stationary and the book was moving in relation to them. Thus, the book appeared to move.

MORE FUN WITH MOTION!

The next time you travel in a moving vehicle, such as a car, a train, or a boat, compare your motion with different frames of reference, such as stationary objects in the vehicle (people, seats, or books) and stationary objects outside the vehicle (trees or buildings).

BOOK LIST

Cwiklik, Robert. *Albert Einstein and the Theory of Relativity.* Hauppauge, N.Y.: Barron's, 1987. A dramatic story about Einstein's life and his discoveries.

Gilbert, Harry, and Diana Gilbert Smith. *Gravity, the Glue of the Universe: History and Activities.* Englewood, Colo.: Teacher Ideas Press, 1997. The history of and activities about scientists and facts related to gravity.

VanCleave, Janice. *Physics for Every Kid.* New York: Wiley, 1991. Fun, simple physics experiments, including information about energy and matter.

II

SCIENTISTS

6

Alhazen

Alhazen (965–1039) was born in 965 in Persia, Basrah (present-day Iraq) and received his education in Basrah and Baghdad. His work on optics was so extensive and detailed that it set the foundation used by many later scientists. The word **optics,** from the Greek *optikes,* originally meant the study of the eye and vision. Today the term refers to the study of all **phenomena** (observable events) related to light. Alhazen was the first to accurately describe the various parts of the eye and to explain the process of vision. In his book *The Treasury of Optics,* Alhazen rejected the earlier Greek idea that the eye sends out rays of light to the object it is looking at. Instead, he correctly suggested that rays of light are reflected off objects and enter the eye.

Under the reign of the Egyptian **caliph** (Muslim ruler) al-Hakim (996–1020), Alhazen led an engineering team to carry out his idea for regulating the flow of the Nile. He soon realized that his plan would not work, and he was fearful that his failure might cost him his life. His fear was based on the fact that al-Hakim was a cruel leader and had done heartless things. Legend has it that he even ordered that all dogs in Cairo be killed because their barking annoyed him. To protect himself, Alhazen pretended to be insane and was confined to his home. During this time, he continued his scientific investigations. After al-Hakim's death, Alhazen was able to show that he had only pretended to be insane. His writings indicate a system of observations (research), hypothesis, and verification by experimentation that was like the scientific method used today. Most other scientists of his day were thinkers, not experimenters.

Alhazen conducted investigations on the transmission of light and colors, optical illusions, and reflections. He examined the **refraction** of light, which is the change in direction of light rays as they pass from one transparent material to another, such as from air to water or from air through a lens. He also carried out the first recorded experiments on the splitting of white light into the **spectrum** (a band of colors, in the order of red, orange, yellow, green, blue, indigo, and violet, produced by separating white light). Alhazen's discoveries about light resulted in great progress in experimental methods and influenced other scientists, including the famous artist and scientist Leonardo da Vinci (1452–1519). The first correct explanation of the light spectrum was given in 1666 by the English mathematician and physicist Sir Isaac Newton.

Alhazen was the first person to develop the **camera obscura** (a device that produces the temporary image of an object). *Camera obscura* comes from Latin and means "dark chamber." Alhazen's camera obscura was a dark room with a hole in one wall. Light passing through this hole acted like light passing through a **convex lens** (a lens with outward curved sides that is thicker in the middle than at the edges), in that it produced an **inverted** (upside-down) image if projected onto a screen, such as the wall opposite the hole. Alhazen used his camera obscura to study a solar eclipse. This allowed him to study the Sun's image without looking directly at the Sun.

Optics were only a small part of the work done by Alhazen. He investigated the relationship between the density of Earth's atmosphere and its height, as well as how the density of the atmosphere affected the refraction of sunlight. He determined that **twilight** (the small amount of light at daybreak or sundown) was due to the refraction of the Sun's light in Earth's atmosphere. Alhazen is said to have written more than 200 books, very few of which have survived.

FUN TIME!
Purpose

To separate the colors that make up white light.

Materials

10-ounce (300-mL) transparent plastic cup
tap water
unlined, white index card

Procedure

1. Fill the cup half full with water.

2. Stand outdoors in a sunny area with the Sun behind you.

3. Hold the cup so that sunlight passes through the water.

4. Position the index card about 4 inches (10 cm) from the cup on the side of the cup opposite the Sun. Tilt the cup toward the card until a rainbow is seen on the card in the cup's shadow.

Results

Flickering, rainbow-colored, dancing bands of light will appear on the card.

Why?

The water and the plastic wall of the cup act like a prism. A **prism** is a triangular-shaped piece of **transparent** (allows light to pass through) material that refracts the rays of white light passing through it so that the light separates into different colors, called the spectrum. A slight motion of the cup causes the water to move back and forth, thus creating the dancing bands of colored lights.

MORE FUN WITH OPTICS

A camera obscura doesn't have to be a room. You can make this simple camera by using an empty cardboard toilet tissue tube. Cover one end of the tube with a 4-inch (10-cm) square piece of waxed paper. Secure the paper with a rubber band. Make an effort to keep the waxed paper as smooth as possible. Cover the open end with a 4-inch (10-cm) square of aluminum foil. Secure the foil with a rubber band. Make a small hole in the center of the foil with a pushpin. Lay the cardboard tube on its side, with the foil-covered end at one of the short sides of a sheet of black construction paper. Tightly wrap the black paper around the cardboard tube, making the longest possible paper tube. Secure the black paper tube with tape. During the day, hold the foil-covered end of the camera toward an open window that is not receiving direct sunlight. Close one eye and look into the black paper tube with your other eye. The waxed paper makes a screen for upside-down images of the outdoors. *Caution: Do not look directly at the Sun through your camera because its brightness can permanently damage your eyes.*

BOOK LIST

Bennett, Carolyn. *Kaleidoscopes.* New York: Workman Publishing, 1994. Activities and information about color, light, and vision, including how to make a kaleidoscope.

Reid, Struan, and Patricia Fara. *The Usborne Book of Scientists.* New York: Scholastic Inc., 1992. Facts about scientists, including Alhazen.

VanCleave, Janice. *Physics for Every Kid.* New York: Wiley, 1991. Fun, simple physics experiments, including information about light.

7

Mary Anning

The British scientist Mary Anning (1799–1847) is one of the first recognized women paleontologists. Mary was also one of the first professional fossil collectors, which means that she sold many of her finds, rather than just keeping a personal collection. At the time of her first discoveries, she was not considered a scientist because she was a young girl with no formal scientific training. Mary learned about fossils from her father. A scientist doesn't necessarily have to have special training, be a certain age, or be a man. Instead, like Mary, a scientist is anyone who searches for answers to scientific questions.

Little is known about Mary Anning's life that isn't connected to her fossil hunting. She was born to Richard and Mary Anning in Lyme Regis, a coastal village on the southern shores of Great Britain. The chalklike cliffs at Lyme Regis were and still are rich in fossils. Many report that only Mary and her father collected the fossils, but some say it was a family activity. Some of the fossils were sold, which added to the small income that Mary's father made as a cabinetmaker, and this helped to support the family. There had been many children in the family, but only two, Mary and her brother Richard, lived to be adults. A family dog also assisted in the fossil hunting. It is not known when the dog became part of the team, but it helped when Mary hunted alone. The dog would sometimes stay to mark the spot of finds that were too big for Mary to carry, while she went for help. The dog is said to have been killed in a rockfall.

Until the early nineteenth century, there was little scientific interest in or understanding of fossils. The English scientist Gideon Mantell (1790–1852) is generally given credit for the discovery in 1822 of one of the earliest recognizable dinosaur fossils, the *iguanodon,* meaning "iguana-tooth." **Dinosaurs** are **extinct** (no longer in existence) reptiles that did not live in water or fly. In other words, dinosaurs were land dwellers. Mantell called Anning "the geological Lioness" because she was so determined in her work. Others called her "the Princess of Paleontology" because of her contributions, mainly in the form of specimens, to this relatively new science.

When Mary was 11, her father died, and the money that Mary and her family made by selling fossils became the family's only income. The family lived in poverty and anonymity (unknown) until the early 1820s, when they met the professional fossil collector Lt. Col. Thomas Birch. Birch sympathized with their desperate financial situation and decided to sell all of his fine fossil collection and donate the money to the Anning family. By the middle of the 1820s, Anning took charge of the family fossil business (her brother had his own career in upholstery and no longer collected fossils). With Birch's help, Anning's family built both a reputation and a business as fossil hunters. These fossils were eagerly sought after, not only by museums and scientists but also by wealthy private collectors and curious tourists. However, although the *Tyrannosaurus rex* skeleton called Sue, which is now in the Field Museum in Chicago, recently fetched millions of dollars, Anning received only small payments for her fossils.

Since Anning sold her fossils, she was given little to no credit for finding them because, generally, museums tended to credit only people who donated the fossils to the institution.

At 12, according to some reports, Anning became the first person to find a nearly complete skeleton of an extinct reptile called the *ichthyosaurus,* which means fish reptile. Others say that Mary's brother Richard made the find and Mary did the digging. But Anning did find many ichthyosaur skeletons that were not as complete. At 25, she made her most important find, which was an almost-complete skeleton of the first ever to be found *plesiosaurus,* which means ribbon lizard. Before this discovery, other scientists thought that animals like this might have existed in times past but they had no proof. Anning provided this proof, which helped to establish her as a respected **fossilist** (a person who is very knowledgeable about fossils).

While she was never given credit for all of her finds, in the last decade of her life she received an annuity (payments) from the British Association for the Advancement of Science (1838). One year before her death from breast cancer, she was named the first Honorary Member of the new Dorset County Museum. Her obituary was published in the *Quarterly Journal of the Geological Society.* The Geological Society was an organization that would not admit women until 1904.

Today more recognition is being given to modern women scientists, and more research is being done to find out about the work of women scientists of the past, such as Mary Anning. For example, researchers today are trying to identify any of Anning's finds that may be in museums or private collections.

FUN TIME!

Purpose

To make a model of fossil bones.

Materials

3-ounce (90-mL) paper cup full of plaster of paris

5-ounce (150-mL) paper cup

5 tablespoons (45 mL) tap water

2 wooden craft sticks (plastic spoons will also work)

7-inch (17.5-cm) paper or plastic plate

24-inch (60-cm), or longer, dried twig

Procedure

1. Pour the plaster of paris into the 5-ounce (150-mL) paper cup.

2. Add the water to the cup, and use one of the craft sticks to stir the mixture until it is a thick paste. Add more water if all the plaster is not wet.

3. Using the same stick, dip out the paste and put it on the plate. Use the second stick to scrape the plaster from the dipping stick.

4. Using one of the sticks, smooth the paste so that it is as even a depth as possible on the plate.

5. Break a piece about 6 inches (15 cm) long from the twig and lay it on the paste on the plate. Press about half of the piece of twig into the paste.

6. Repeat step 5, using different-length pieces broken from the twig to form a shape like a fish.

7. Allow the paste to dry.

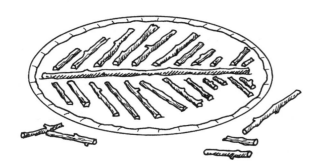

Results

A model of fossil bones of a fish is made.

Why?

The word fossil comes from the Latin word *fossilis,* meaning "dug up." Today, a fossil means the traces of any past life preserved in rock. The model in this activity represents fossil bones of a fish that have been covered in rock. The rock (plaster) covering the bones (twig pieces) has **eroded** (broken and moved away) so that the bones are visible. Anning would have been able to find many such fossils on the Lyme Regis coast because of its unique geological features. This area was and still is rich with fossils that are brought to the surface as the water from the ocean breaks up the rocky shore.

When an animal dies, its body usually **decays** (naturally breaks down) in time, leaving no recognizable trace. But if the body is quickly covered with **sediment** (rock, sand, or dirt that has been carried to a place by water, wind, or ice), water containing chemicals can seep through the sediment and into the animal's bones and teeth. When the water evaporates, some of the chemicals in the water are left behind, sticking the sediment together and filling the spaces in the bone. Slowly, the sediment turns to rock, and the bones become fossilized.

MORE FUN WITH FOSSILS!

Dinosaurs lived between 230 and 65 million years ago. Paleontologists use the bones that they find to make educated guesses about what dinosaurs looked liked. Use the skeleton shown here and your imagination to draw a dinosaur. You can place a sheet of paper over the skeleton diagram and use the skeleton as a guide to draw your dinosaur. Paleontologists name their fossil finds by combining Latin and

Greek root words to describe the animal by its likely appearance and behavior. For example, *Tyrannosaurus rex* means "tyrant lizard king." The name can also include where the fossil was found or even the name of the scientist who made the discovery. The following list can be used to help you name your own imaginary dinosaur.

BOOK LIST

Benton, Michael. *Dinosaur and Other Prehistoric Animal Fact Finder.* New York: Kingfisher Books, 1992. Information about prehistoric animals and how their bones were preserved.

Stille, Darlene. *Extraordinary Women Scientists.* Chicago: Childrens Press, 1995. Biographies of women scientists, including Mary Anning.

VanCleave, Janice. *Dinosaurs for Every Kid.* New York: Wiley, 1993. Fun facts and investigations about dinosaurs, including information about their fossil remains and how they are named.

Dinosaur Name Chart

Name	Meaning	Name	Meaning
ankylo	crooked	mega	large
anuro	no tail	micro	small
bary	heavy	mono	one
brachio	arm	pachy	thick
cephalo	head	pod	foot
ceros	horn	rex	king
compso	pretty	saur, saurus	lizard
di	two	tri	three
dino	terrible	tyranno	tyrant
masso	bulk, body	veloci	speedy

8

Archimedes

The Greek mathematician and physicist Archimedes (287–212 B.C.) was born in Syracuse, Sicily, and was educated in Alexandria, Egypt. Little is known about Archimedes' childhood except that his father was an astronomer. We know a bit more about his adult life from the prefaces to some of his writings and a few stories written by others. In one amusing story, he described sending math ideas to his mathematician friends in Alexandria. He was surprised when some of those who had received the ideas claimed them as their own. Archimedes suspected that these men did not really understand the ideas, so, to expose them, he sent more ideas but included two that he knew to be incorrect. No mention is made of the results, but Archimedes' plan was that the dishonest mathematicians would be discredited for promoting false ideas.

In another story, Archimedes was asked by the king to discover whether the king's crown was made of pure gold. The king had given a goldsmith a specific amount of gold to make a crown. He had heard that the goldsmith was trying to cheat him by not using all of the gold in the crown. Instead, he might have used a mixture of gold and silver. The gold and silver crown weighed as much as the gold given him to use. How could Archimedes figure out if the crown was pure gold or not?

Archimedes was a very observant person, and one day while taking a bath, he is said to have noticed that when he got into the full tub, some of the water was pushed out. He realized that his body had **displaced** (taken the place of something) the water in the tub and that the amount of displacement had to do with his body's volume. That meant he could determine the volume of the king's crown by water displacement. Archimedes knew that silver was lighter than an equal volume of gold, so for an object made of a mixture of silver and gold to weigh as much as a pure gold object, more of the silver/gold mixture would have to be used. This would mean that a crown of gold and silver mixed would be larger than one made of pure gold that had the same weight. Archimedes weighed the crown in question by balancing it with a piece of gold. He then lowered the gold into a container of water and marked how high the water rose. When he did the same with the crown, the crown caused the water to rise higher than it had when the gold was in it, indicating that the crown had a greater volume than the gold did. Therefore, the crown was not made of pure gold, and the goldsmith had stolen gold from the king.

The most unlikely part of this story is that when Archimedes discovered how to solve the king's problem, he became so excited that he jumped from his bath and ran naked through the streets, screaming "Eureka!" (I've got it!).

Archimedes was also known for inventing new war machines that managed to hold off Roman soldiers who were attacking his city. These machines included lenses that focused sunlight onto ships, causing them to catch on fire, and pulleys that were used in special machines that could lift and overturn invading ships. It is said that Archimedes' death came about because he was so absorbed in working on a math diagram that he didn't realize that the Romans had finally broken through the city's defenses. When an enemy soldier entered his room and demanded that Archimedes come with him, Archimedes paid no attention and commanded the intruder not to mess up the diagrams that he was drawing. The insulted soldier drew his sword and killed Archimedes.

One **principle** (a basic truth, law, rule, or belief) that resulted from Archimedes' bathing discovery is now called Archimedes' Principle. This principle is that an object in a **fluid** (a gas or a liquid) is lifted by **buoyancy** (the upward force of a fluid on an object placed in it). The buoyancy of an object is equal to the weight of the fluid displaced by the object. This principle applies to both floating and **submerged** (sunken or pushed beneath the surface of a fluid) objects and to all fluids, and it explains why boats float. (See chapter 16, "Galileo Galilei," for information about the effect of buoyancy on falling objects.)

FUN TIME!

Purpose

To determine how much cargo a boat can hold and still float.

Materials

large deep bowl
tap water
75 pennies
5-ounce (150-mL) paper cup
paper towel
food scale with gram measurements

Procedure

1. Fill the bowl about three-fourths full with water.

2. Place 10 coins in the paper cup, then place the cup in the water. The cup should float upright.

3. Add coins 1 at a time to the cup until 1 coin makes the cup sink.

4. Remove the cup from the water and pour out the water. Dry the coins with the paper towel.

5. Remove 1 coin and determine the mass in grams of the remaining coins by using the food scale.

6. Compare the mass of the coins with the milliliter volume of the cup.

Results

The mass of the coins in grams will equal or nearly equal the milliliter volume of the cup.

Why?

Just before it sank, the top of the cup was level with the surface of the water. In this position, the cup displaced (pushed aside) the amount of water equal to the volume of the cup. An object will float as long as its mass in grams is equal to the volume of water it displaces in milliliters. This is true because the density of water is 1 g/1 mL, which means that 1 gram of water has a volume of 1 milliliter. In this experiment, the cup will float as long as the mass of the cup in grams is not greater than the volume of the cup in milliliters. Like the cup, a boat will float as long as the mass of the boat and its cargo in grams isn't greater than the volume of water that the boat displaces in milliliters.

MORE FUN WITH BUOYANCY!

The comparison of the mass of an object to its volume is called density. An object floats in water if its density is less than the density of water. The density of gases is much less than the density of water. Life preservers are generally made of materials with air trapped in them. These pockets of air decrease the density of the material, thus increasing its **buoyancy** (ability to float). You can show how adding a gas to an object can change its density and thus its buoyancy. Fill a 9-ounce (270-mL) clear plastic cup with a colorless soda. Open a small bag of herbal tea, such as orange spice tea, and pour the tea into the plastic cup. Use a spoon to gently stir the contents of the cup. Observe the contents by viewing the cup from the side. Note that most of the tea leaves float on the surface of the soda, but some leaves first sink and then rise as bubbles of gas collect on them, then sink again as the bubbles are knocked off at the surface. Soda contains bubbles of carbon dioxide gas, the same gas that is in your exhaled breath. When the gas becomes attached to the tea leaves, it increases their buoyancy, so they float to the top of the soda.

BOOK LIST

Clements, Gillian. *The Picture History of Great Inventors*.
New York: Knopf, 1994. The contributions of inventors
and engineers from the earliest civilizations to the present
day.

Graham, Ian. *Boats, Ships, Submarines, and Other Floating
Machines*. New York: Kingfisher Books, 1993. Information,
experiments, and activities about different kinds of boats
and how they work.

Kentley, Eric. *Boat*. New York: Dorling Kindersley Eyewitness
Books, 1992. A history of the development and uses of boats
and ships, from ancient birch-bark canoes to modern luxury
liners.

VanCleave, Janice. *Physics for Every Kid*. New York: Wiley,
1990. A collection of fun experiments about physics topics,
including buoyancy.

Wiese, Jim. *Rocket Science*. New York: Wiley, 1995.
Experiments and information about moving machines,
including boats.

9

Alexander Graham Bell

Alexander Graham Bell (1847–1922) was born in Edinburgh, Scotland. Alexander was the middle son of Alexander Melville Bell and Eliza Grace Symonds. His mother was a portrait painter and an accomplished musician. She was hard of hearing, but with the help of an ear tube, which was a cone-shaped tube with the smaller end held in her ear, she could hear some sounds. Alexander's father was a well-known teacher and author of textbooks on correct speech, as well as the inventor of "visible speech" (a code of symbols that indi-cated the position and the action of the throat, the tongue, and the lips in uttering various sounds), which helped hearing-impaired people speak.

Alexander and his two brothers assisted their father in giving public demonstrations of visual speech. People in the audience would suggest words or sounds, such as a barking dog or a birdcall. Melville would write down his coded symbols for the words or sounds; then the boys would come onstage, read the symbols, and make the sounds.

The young Alexander was also very interested in learning about the human ability to hear and speak. He and his brothers made a model of the human skull with vocal parts that when attached to a **bellows** (a device whose sides are squeezed to pump out air) could scream "Mama." Alexander also taught his dog to growl steadily while he manipulated the dog's mouth and throat. As he did this, the dog seemed to say, "Ow ah oo, ga-ma-ma," meaning, "How are you, Grandmother?"

By 1870, both of Alexander's brothers had died of **tuberculosis** (a lung disease), and his parents moved to Brantford, Ontario, Canada, which they believed had a healthier climate. In 1871, Alexander moved to Boston to pursue his goal of helping the deaf by opening a school for teachers of the deaf. This school later became part of Boston University, and Alexander became a professor of **vocal physiology** (the study of how the body produces sound) and **elocution** (the art of speaking clearly).

Bell had been experimenting with sound most of his life, but the invention for which he is best known is the telephone. While he was trying to invent a telegraph that could carry several messages at the same time, he remembered how singing into a piano caused the strings to vibrate. This gave him the idea that speech could be transmitted and received over electric wires. He didn't know enough about electric devices to put his idea into practice, so in 1875 he hired Thomas Watson, who worked in an electrical shop, to help him. On March 10, 1876, after they'd been working on the invention for some time, Bell accidentally spilled acid on his clothes and shouted, "Mr. Watson, come here. I want to see you." Watson, who was in another room, heard this now-famous sentence through the speaker of the invention. Bell decided to call his invention a telephone. *Telephone* is from the Greek word

tele for "far off" and *phone* for "sound." By July 1876, the Bell Telephone Company was in business. Within 10 years, there were over 150,000 telephones in the United States.

The year following his invention of the telephone, Bell married Mabel Hubbard, a deaf student whom he had taught to speak in his class. With income from his telephone invention, Bell was able to spend his life working on other inventions and helping the deaf.

Bell met six-year-old Helen Keller in 1887. Helen was both deaf and blind. Bell directed Helen's parents to a school where they met Anne Sullivan, the teacher who taught Helen how to communicate with other people. Helen and Bell remained friends throughout his life and worked together to help people with disabilities. In order to communicate with Helen, Bell learned sign language (a language in which hand gestures are used to stand for different words of speech and also to represent the letters of the alphabet) and **braille** (a system of writing for blind people, using raised dots for letters that one "reads" by feeling these with the fingertips). Helen could "hear" by feeling a person's lips, as well as by feeling someone's hand signals with her hands. She could "speak" by signing, but by the age of 10 she had also learned to speak out loud.

FUN TIME!

Purpose

To produce a string telephone.

Materials

pencil
two 5-ounce (150-mL) paper cups
20 feet (6 m) of #10 crochet string
2 small metal paper clips
helper

Procedure

1. Use the pencil to make a small hole in the bottom of one of the cups.

2. Thread the end of the string through the hole and into the cup. Tie this end of the string to one of the paper clips.

3. Repeat steps 1 and 2, using the free end of the string and the remaining cup and paper clip.

4. With you holding one cup and your helper holding the other, walk away from each other so that the string attached to the cups is tight.

5. Ask your helper to hold the cup over his or her ear as you speak into your cup. Repeat this step by holding the cup over your ear and asking your helper to speak into his or her cup.

Results

The person with the cup over his or her ear hears what is being said into the other cup.

Why?

Sounds are made when things, such as the string and the cup in this experiment, **vibrate** (rapidly move up and down or back and forth). In this experiment, the vibrations of the speaker's voice make one cup vibrate. These vibrations travel along the string to the other cup, which vibrates and the speaker's voice is heard. A telephone works not because the telephone wire vibrates but because the vibrations of voice sounds are changed into electrical signals. The signals travel along wires from the mouthpiece of one telephone to the earpiece of another telephone, where the signals are changed back into sound.

MORE FUN WITH COMMUNICATION!

In American Sign Language, signers use a combination of hand shape, hand orientation, hand location, and hand movement to form words and convey meaning. People who use sign language sometimes spell out words, signing letters of the alphabet with their fingers. The American Manual Alphabet shown here is the finger-spelling system most commonly used in the United States. Practice forming each letter with your hand, then memorize the sign for the alphabet. Practice signing your name and other words.

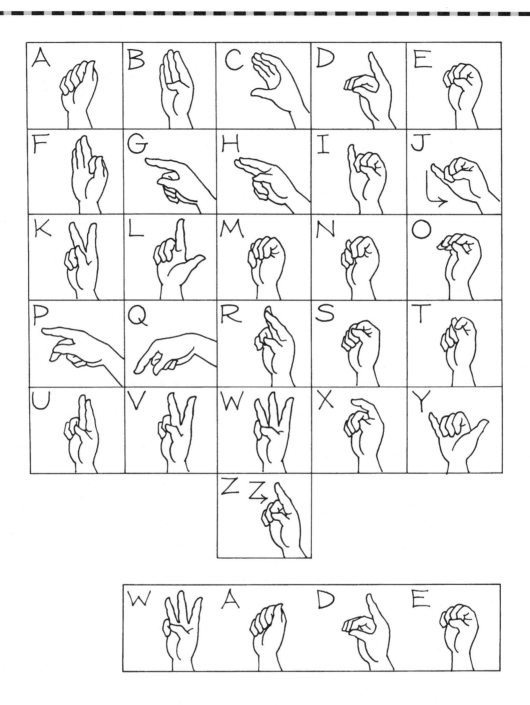

BOOK LIST

Colombo, Luann. *Beakman's Book of Dead Guys and Gals of Science.* Kansas City, Mo.: Andrews and McMeel, 1994. Short biographies and time lines of the lives of famous scientists of the past, including Alexander Graham Bell.

MacLeod, Elizabeth. *Alexander Graham Bell: An Inventive Life.* New York: Scholastic, 1999. A biography of Alexander Graham Bell.

Pollard, Michael and Philip Wilkinson. *Scientists Who Changed the World.* New York: Chelsea House, 1994. Facts about the well-known and not so well-known scientists who have made a difference in scientific advancements.

Sullivan, George. *Helen Keller.* New York: Scholastic, 2000. A biography of Helen Keller, including stories in Helen's own words.

VanCleave, Janice. *The Human Body for Every Kid.* New York: Wiley, 1995. Fun, simple science experiments, including information about how you hear sounds.

10

Rachel Carson

Rachel Carson (1907–1964), an American scientist and writer, has been called the mother of the modern environmental movement. She credited her mother, Maria, with introducing her to the world of nature, which became her lifelong passion.

Rachel, the youngest of three children, was born in Springdale, near Pittsburgh, Pennsylvania. Her father, Robert, was an insurance salesman. The Carson home was in the country, and like many houses at that time, it had no gas, electricity, or running water. The family used oil lamps or candles for lighting, a wood-burning fireplace to provide heat, and a wood-burning stove for cooking.

Rachel's mother had been a teacher before she married. In those days, unmarried, educated women worked mainly as teachers, librarians, or secretaries. But a married woman was expected to stay home and take care of her family. So Mrs. Carson taught piano in order to provide additional money for the family. Mrs. Carson and Rachel also spent a lot of time studying the wildlife near their home. Rachel began to collect living things and, in response to her mother's training, always treated living creatures with care. Mrs. Carson did not always answer Rachel's many questions; instead she encouraged her daughter to discover the answers for herself. This taught Rachel how to research, think things through, and explain the results to others. It was great training for Rachel's future career as a scientist and a writer.

Carson's grades in high school won her a college scholarship to Pennsylvania College for Women. She entered college with the dream of being a professional writer. But in her sophomore year, she took a course in biology, which changed the direction of her life. At that time, although there were a few women science teachers and professors, women were generally discouraged from becoming working scientists. But Carson's biology professor, Mary Scott Skinker, insisted that women could excel just as well as men in science. Mary inspired Carson to become a biologist.

Carson graduated with honors and went to Johns Hopkins University in Baltimore, Maryland, to work on a master's degree in zoology. She wanted to be a marine biologist and to study the life in the sea. She began her studies in 1929, the first year of the Great Depression. It was a time when getting a job was difficult, especially for women. Carson had a scholarship that paid for her first year of schooling, but after that, she had to work to pay her tuition. Later, male classmates confessed that they didn't think a woman could work more than one job and still get top grades, especially in science. But they were wrong. Carson worked two and sometimes three jobs and got her master's degree in zoology in the spring of 1932.

Even with her degree, Carson could not find a job as a marine biologist because she was a woman. So she took any job she could get, including writing articles for newspapers

and teaching zoology at the University of Maryland. In the summertime, Carson studied at the Marine Biological Laboratories in Woods Hole, Massachusetts. It was here that she began to develop her deep love of the sea.

Carson's life changed drastically in 1935 when her father died. She now had her mother to support. Then in 1936 her sister died, leaving two young children. Carson needed a better-paying job to support her family. She applied for a job as a junior aquatic biologist with the U.S. Bureau of Fisheries. She was the first of two women hired by the bureau for a nonclerical job. Although her title was "biologist," she did not work in a laboratory or on a scientific research ship. Actually, her job was to write radio scripts about fish and other forms of marine life. These were part of a radio series about marine animals called *Romance under the Waters*. In time, she became the chief editor of all publications for the U.S. Fish and Wildlife Service (a later name for the U.S. Bureau of Fisheries). Carson's job allowed her to explore life under the sea and to do some writing on the side.

In 1937, the *Atlantic Monthly* magazine published an article by Carson, called "Undersea." This publication became the basis for Carson's first book, *Under the Sea Wind*. It was published in 1941, one month before the United States entered World War II, so people were focused on world politics and were not interested in reading a book about the ocean. After the war ended in 1945, Carson edited and even wrote some of the booklets in a series called *Conservation in Action*. Because of the information in these booklets, Carson started to worry about the environment but at this time was not aware of any serious problems. She was interested in writing a book about the sea that would be not only informative but interesting and understandable to everyone.

In 1949, Carson took a leave of absence from her job to study life in the Atlantic Ocean from a U.S. Fish and Wildlife Service survey ship. She began work on what would become her first best-seller, *The Sea around Us*. Because of the book's popularity, Carson was able to resign from the U.S. Fish and Wildlife Service and devote her time to writing. She wrote two more books about the sea. All of her books were very successful and are still in print, but it was her interest in the dangers of pesticides that made her one of the most influential women of our time. Carson became interested in the effects of pesticides when a friend with a private bird sanctuary asked for Carson's help. Her friend explained that in an effort to kill mosquitoes, a plane had sprayed DDT, a powerful pesticide, over the sanctuary. As a result, many birds and harmless insects were killed. In order to bring the problem to the public's attention, Carson decided to write a book about it. During her research for the book, she collected facts from experts around the world. She was shocked at what she discovered. For example, the pesticide called DDT caused many problems in animals, including the loss of calcium from the shells of bird eggs. This loss caused the eggs to be soft and easily cracked, preventing baby birds from developing.

In 1962, *Silent Spring* was published. The title suggested that if pollution was not stopped, it would someday result in a silent spring, one without the beautiful sounds of birds and other creatures. Carson hoped that the book would encourage people to make changes in the use of pesticides before many more animals died. Her book did not please everyone. Some accused her of being a hysterical woman who was exaggerating the issue. But many others praised her for trying to make people face a serious problem. The book resulted in President John F. Kennedy's appointing a committee to study pesticides. Although the committee agreed with many of Carson's findings, it was not until 1972 that government action was taken and DDT was banned (forbidden to be used) in the United States. Many other nations have also banned it or put it under strict control.

Carson never married, but she did adopt the son of her niece after her niece died. Rachel died of cancer in 1964, but her efforts as an ecologist to make the world a safer place live on.

FUN TIME!

Purpose

To observe what happens when calcium is removed from eggshells.

Materials

1 raw egg in its shell
petroleum jelly
3 cups (750 mL) white vinegar
1-quart (1-L) bowl

Procedure

Caution: Wash your hands after you touch raw eggs. Eggs can contain bacteria that can make you ill.

1. Carefully feel the egg without breaking the shell. Notice how firm the shell feels.

2. Cover one-half of the eggshell with a thick layer of petroleum jelly.

3. Pour the vinegar into the bowl.

4. Gently place the egg in the bowl so as not to crack the shell.

5. Each day for 3 days, lift the egg out of the vinegar and examine the firmness of the shell on the petroleum-covered and the uncovered sides. Wash your hands with soap and water after each examination.

petroleum jelly

White Vinegar

Results

At first, the uncovered section of the shell is covered with bubbles; then this part of the shell becomes thin and disappears.

Why?

Eggshells contain a chemical called calcium carbonate. This chemical makes eggshells firm. In this experiment, a chemical reaction results from combining vinegar (an acid) and calcium carbonate. The visible product, the bubbles seen on the egg, is the gas carbon dioxide. As the calcium carbonate is removed, the shell becomes thinner and finally disappears. Where the shell is covered with petroleum, the vinegar does not mix with the calcium carbonate, so the shell does not change.

MORE FUN WITH EGGS!

Can you make a rubber egg? Carefully place a raw egg in its shell in a quart jar. Then cover the egg with white vinegar. Allow the egg to remain in the vinegar undisturbed for two days

or until the entire eggshell disappears. Use a spoon to carefully take the egg out of the vinegar. Rinse the egg with water. Hold the egg over a bowl and feel it. Try to bounce the egg in the bowl. Although the egg may act a bit rubbery, the egg has not turned to rubber, and the thin covering around the egg can break. (Note: Occasionally, the covering around the egg will break before the egg is removed from the vinegar. If this happens, try it again with another egg.)

vinegar

BOOK LIST

Bernstein, Leonard. *Multicultural Women of Science.* Maywood, N.J.: Peoples Publishing Group, Inc., 1996. Contributions of women scientists, including Rachel Carson.

Haven, Kendall, and Donna Clark. *100 Most Popular Scientists for Young Adults.* Englewood, Colo.: Libraries Unlimited, Inc., 1999. Biographical sketches of scientists, including Rachel Carson.

Sabin, Francene. *Rachel Carson.* New York: Troll, 1993. Describes the life of the marine biologist and science writer Rachel Carson, whose book *Silent Spring* changed the way we look at pesticides.

VanCleave, Janice. *Ecology for Every Kid.* New York: Wiley, 1996. Fun facts and investigations about ecology.

11

Marie and Pierre Curie

The Polish physicist Marie Curie (1867–1934) was one of the first women scientists to win worldwide fame. She was born Marya Sklodowska in Warsaw, Poland. Her eldest sister died when Marya was eight, and her mother died two years later. Her father, a physics and math teacher, had a hard time supporting his family because Warsaw was under Russian rule, and the Russians replaced many Polish teachers with Russian teachers.

Marya was the youngest of five children. She was very intelligent, loved to learn, and did well at school. At that time women were not allowed to attend Polish universities, so Marya's education would have ended after high school if it hadn't been for her sister. Marya and her sister, Bronya, made a pact that they would help each other to continue their education. It was decided that Bronya would study medicine in Paris while Marya went to work and supported her. Marya worked in Poland as a governess for six years, sending money to Bronya in Paris, while she continued to study chemistry and mathematics privately.

In 1891, it was Marya's turn to attend college. She enrolled at the University of Paris and changed her name to Marie. Because she had little money, Marie rented a small room without electricity or water. She had to climb six flights of stairs to get to her room, and many days she ate only bread and drank hot chocolate. But by 1894, Marie had degrees in physics and mathematics. In that same year, Marie met Pierre Curie (1859–1906), a professor of physics. They married in 1895 but were too poor to purchase rings. For their honeymoon, they took a bicycle tour. Bicycling was a sport that they enjoyed throughout their life together.

By the end of the nineteenth century, some thought that all that could be learned about chemistry and physics had been discovered. But in the last years of the nineteenth century, scientists began to make exciting new discoveries about atoms. For example, in 1896, the French physicist Antoine-Henri Becquerel (1852–1908) discovered that an energy given off by the element uranium would affect a photographic plate in a similar way as light. This meant that the energy from uranium, like light, is a form of **radiation** (energy that can move through space and that is not carried by matter). Becquerel also discovered that uranium causes the air around it to have an electrical charge. Becquerel was a pioneer in **nuclear physics,** which is the study of the nucleus (the central part) of an atom.

In 1897, Marie went back to school to get an advanced degree in physics. To earn this degree, she had to make a scientific discovery or solve a scientific problem. She decided to learn more about the energy given off by uranium. Using a device that Pierre invented, Marie was able to measure the electrical charge around uranium and other samples. She discovered that another element, thorium, gives off radiation. Marie named this spontaneous process of **emission** (the release of something) of radiation radioactivity. She also discovered that a black rock called pitchblende was radioactive and thus must contain one or more radioactive elements. Pierre joined his wife in searching for radioactive elements in pitchblende. One of the elements was thorium, but they also discovered two new radioactive elements. Marie named one of the elements *radium* (after the energy being emitted) and the other *polonium* (after her home country, Poland).

The Curies separated the radioactive elements from pitchblende by heating the rock and then letting the gases that formed **condense** (change from a gas to a liquid). Most of the liquid that condensed was not radioactive and was discarded. It took more than 1,000 pounds (454 kg) of pitchblende to produce less than 0.0035 ounce (0.1 g) of radium. Had the Curies patented their method of removing the radium, they would have been very wealthy, but they thought that the work of scientists should be available to everyone. As scientists, they thought that the government would provide support. They were not taken care of, however, and Marie did not receive any pay for her work or have proper laboratory equipment to work with until after she became famous.

The atoms of the radioactive elements that the Curies worked with decayed (the spontaneous change of the nucleus of a radioactive element into another nucleus). During the decay, radioactive particles are given off, which can cause other substances to **luminesce** (give off light). Bottles of radioactive materials lined the shelves in the Curies' laboratory, as well as in their home. They were fascinated that these bottles glowed in the dark. No one, including the Curies, knew that radioactive material might be deadly. When both Marie and Pierre started feeling tired and ill soon after working with the radioactive materials, they did suspect that the radioactive materials had caused their illness. However, they never stopped their work or changed how they handled the materials.

In 1903, Marie received her doctorate in physics and became the first woman in Europe to receive such a degree. In the same year, Marie, Pierre, and Becquerel shared the Nobel Prize for their work, but the Curies were too ill from what is now known as radiation poisoning to travel to Sweden to accept the prize. Marie was the first woman to receive a Nobel Prize.

In 1906, being weak and tired, Pierre fell and was run over and killed by a horse-drawn wagon. Two years later, Marie took over Pierre's teaching position at the University of Paris, becoming the first woman professor in the history of the university. Marie achieved many more firsts in her life. She is the only woman to date who has received two Nobel Prizes (one in physics in 1903 and the second in chemistry in 1911). She is also the only woman whose daughter (Irène Joliot-Curie,

1897–1956) also won a Nobel Prize (in chemistry in 1935).

Marie Curie died from **leukemia** (cancer of the blood), caused by exposure to radiation. She became the first woman to be buried under the famous dome of the Pantheon in Paris. In 1956, Irène, like her mother, died of leukemia as a result of working with radioactive materials.

FUN TIME!

Purpose

To model how scientists can determine what's happening inside an atom.

Materials

sheet of white copy paper
transparent tape
book at least 1 inch (2.5 cm) thick
ruler
can of tuna or other can of food of a comparable height
paper plate
marble

Procedure

1. Roll the copy paper into a tube so that the diameter of the tube is larger than the marble. Secure the tube with tape.

2. Lay the book near the edge of a table.

3. Using the ruler, set the can of tuna 12 inches (30 cm) in front of the book.

4. Turn the paper plate upside down and place it on the tuna can.

5. Support one end of the paper tube on the book so that it is aimed toward the left edge of the paper plate.

6. Let the marble roll down through the tube.

Observe the path of the marble toward the plate and its path when it exits from beneath the paper plate.

7. Move the paper tube to the right and repeat step 6.

8. Repeat step 7 until you reach the right edge of the plate.

Results

The path of the marble creates a pattern much like the one shown here.

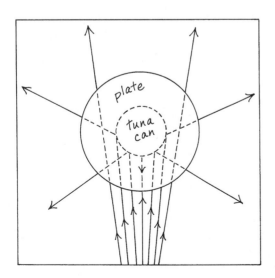

Why?

You cannot see the can under the paper plate, but by rolling the marble under the plate, you can observe the path the marble takes after it goes under the plate. The path of the marble gives a clue as to the shape and the size of the object under the plate. Scientists use a similar technique to study parts of an atom that can't be seen, even with the strongest microscope. With a device called a particle accelerator, tiny particles can be fired at an atom. Scientists observe the paths of these particles and use that information to determine the location, size, and shape of particles inside the atom.

MORE FUN WITH ATOMS!

The change of the nucleus of an atom is called a **nuclear reaction.** One type of nuclear reaction is called **nuclear fission** (the splitting of a large nucleus into two smaller nuclei). For nuclear fission to occur, the nucleus has to be bombarded by particles such as neutrons (uncharged particles inside an atom's nucleus). When a nucleus is split, neutrons inside the nucleus move out and hit the nuclei of other atoms, which causes these nuclei to split, thus releasing more neutrons, which hit other nuclei, and so on. This is called a **chain reaction** (a nuclear reaction in which some of the products of the reaction cause the reaction to keep going).

You can model a chain reaction by using groups of marbles. Lay a cloth towel on a table to keep the marbles from rolling away. Smooth the towel and lay a paper towel on top of it. Position 12 marbles in four different sets of 3 marbles (as shown) on a table. Use a ruler with a groove to launch a "shooter," which will be a marble that represents a neutron. Place one end of the ruler near one set of marbles so that the groove of the ruler is in line with the center of the set of marbles. Raise the opposite end of the ruler. Allow the shooter to roll down the ruler and strike the set of marbles. Marbles from this set should move outward, striking another set of marbles, and so on. If all of the marble sets are not struck, try again, placing the sets in different places.

BOOK LIST

Bernstein, Leonard. *Multicultural Women of Science*. Maywood, N.J.: Peoples Publishing Group, 1996. Biographical sketches of notable women of science, including Marie Curie, with a hands-on activity for each scientist.

Meadows, Jack. *The Great Scientists*. New York: Oxford University Press, 1997. The story of science told through the lives of great scientists, including the Curies.

VanCleave, Janice. *Chemistry for Every Kid*. New York: Wiley, 1989. Fun, simple chemistry experiments, including information about atoms.

Wilkinson, Philip, and Michael Pollard. *Scientists Who Changed the World*. New York: Chelsea House, 1994. Biographies of scientists, including Marie and Pierre Curie.

12

Thomas Alva Edison

Thomas Alva Edison (1847–1931) was born in Milan, Ohio. He was the seventh and last child of Samuel Edison Jr. and Nancy Elliot Edison. His mother was a former schoolteacher; his father had no specific training and was considered a jack-of-all-trades, meaning that he could do many different kinds of jobs. When Thomas was seven, his family moved to Port Huron, Michigan.

Stories of Thomas's childhood differ on the minor facts. But all of the stories agree that from an early age, Thomas was very curious about the world around him, and he tried to teach himself through reading, experimenting, and asking lots of questions. He quizzed everyone about everything. His endless questions annoyed his father, but his mother was much more patient. His first grade teacher also didn't appreciate Thomas's questions. The teacher preferred that students not interrupt him, and he whipped those who did. Once the teacher called Thomas "addled," which means "slow-witted." The following day, Nancy Edison brought Thomas back to school to discuss this comment with his teacher. The teacher told Mrs. Edison that Thomas couldn't learn, and Mrs. Edison became so angry that she took Thomas out of school and decided to teach him herself at home.

Thomas became very interested in science and inventions at an early age and spent a great deal of time experimenting. At age 10, he built his first science laboratory in the basement of the family's home. His father did not approve of all the time that Thomas spent on science, so he paid Thomas a penny for each novel or history book he read. Thomas did the reading, collected the money, and often spent it on supplies for his experiments and inventions.

Thomas had always had ear problems, but at 15, while he was trying to jump onto a moving train, a conductor, in an effort to help, grabbed Thomas's ears to help pull him up. Thomas said that he felt something snap inside his head, and soon he began to lose much of his hearing. Although surgery could have cured his hearing problem, Thomas refused to have it. He is quoted as saying that his deafness helped him to concentrate and encouraged him to read more. He was one of the first people to use the Detroit Free Library. He read all kinds of books, but his favorites were those relating to science and inventions.

The curious boy grew into a curious man and became one of the most **prolific** (productive) American inventors of the nineteenth century. During the 84 years of his life, Edison patented 1,093 inventions. Some things he invented by himself, such as the phonograph in 1877, which was his favorite invention. Other inventions were improvements of things, such as the telegraph. Edison's improved telegraph could transmit 1,000 words a minute, as compared to the earlier models, which had a top speed of 45 words a minute. He created what became known as an invention factory, where he and his workers invented, built, and shipped products. He often required everyone working for him to stay night and day until an invention was completed.

Edison spent all his time thinking about his work, until he became distracted by one of his workers, the 15-year-old Mary Stilwell (1855–1884). Mary was very shy, and since Edison was basically deaf, they had rarely spoken to each other. Then one day he asked her what she thought of him and if she would marry him. During their courtship, the couple had little to no time alone. Usually, they were under the watchful eyes of Mary's parents. Edison is said to have taught Mary Morse code so that he could tap secret messages into the palm of her hand. In a short time, Edison asked Mary's father for permission to marry her. They were married on Christmas Day of 1871. About an hour after the ceremony, Edison remembered something he needed to do at his factory and rushed off. He says that he returned by dinnertime, but others say that he got so involved in his work, he had to be reminded to go home. Edison would at times become so absorbed in working that he did not go home for several days. This behavior continued throughout the marriage.

Edison's work even influenced the nicknames of his children. His daughter, Marion, born in 1873, was nicknamed "Dot," and his son Thomas Jr., born in 1876, was nicknamed "Dash," after the dots and dashes used in Morse code. William Leslie, born in 1878, did not have a nickname.

Edison had seen great changes in the world during his lifetime, and he was responsible for many of them. When he was born in 1847, there was no electricity in homes. In 1878, he formed the Edison Light Company, with the financial support of some of New York's richest businessmen, to research the **electric lamp** (a device that gives off light; commonly called an electric lightbulb). Edison did not yet have a lamp or an electric system, and his investors became impatient waiting for his invention to be created. What was missing from Edison's lamp was the right material for the filament.

The **filament** is the fine thread that gets hot and gives off light in a lamp. Edison needed a material that would get hot but would not melt when a small amount of **electric current** (the flow of electric charges) moved through it. The material also had to be readily available so that his lamps would not be too expensive. Edison tested the fibers from thousands of plants, collected from different parts of the world. He tried many materials and thought of using **tungsten** (a metal that has the highest melting point of all metals), which is used in bulbs today, but at that time he did not have the tools to make a thin thread from this metal. He finally burned a piece of cardboard, producing a thin, hairlike piece of carbon. Carbon is an element that is part of many chemicals, and one found in organisms (living things). It is the black substance, called **soot,** that is left when most things burn. With this as the filament, the lamp burned 170 hours. The emission of light due to the high temperature of an object is called **incandescence.**

Edison's lamp was not the first electric lamp or the first **incandescent** (glowing due to incandescence) lamp, but it was what Edison had promised—a lamp that was practical and cheap. Edison's first commercial lamps were installed on the steamship *Columbia* and later in a New York City factory. With this invention, the age of electricity began.

Before Edison started work on his lamp, he knew that the type of **electric circuit** (the path of an electric current) then in use, called a **series circuit** (a circuit with only one path for the electric current), was not very practical. Lamps in a series are connected one after the other, so that the same electricity that flows through the first lamp goes into the second lamp and so on. Edison's first great idea for electric lighting was that lamps be connected in a **parallel circuit** (a circuit in which the electric current divides and follows two or more paths). The path of the electricity in this type of circuit allowed electricity to flow through different branches, and lamps on one branch could be turned off without affecting lamps on the other branches.

FUN TIME!

Purpose

To determine the effect of removing a lamp from a series circuit.

Materials

size C battery
2 flashlight lamps with screw bases
C battery holder with color-coded wire
  leads
2 flashlight lamp holders with screw bases
wire cutters
4-inch (10-cm) strip of 20-gauge insulated
  single-strand wire
screwdriver (the type that fits terminal
  screws on a lamp holder)
clock or watch

Procedure

Caution: Do not use an electric source other than the one C battery, and disconnect the battery after about 5 seconds. Touching the wires will not shock you, but if the battery is connected for an extended period, the wires will get hot and can burn your fingers.

1. Place the battery and the lamps in their holders.

2. With the wire cutters, strip about ½ inch (1.25 cm) of insulation off each end of the 4-inch (10-cm) wires.

3. Use the wire to connect the two lamp holders by following these steps:
   (a) With the screwdriver, loosen one terminal screw on each lamp holder.

(b) Wrap one metal end of the wire around each terminal and tighten the screws to hold the ends of the wire in place.

4. Follow the instructions in step 3 to connect one of the battery wires to the free terminal of lamp holder A. Observe the lamps.

5. Touch the metal end of the loose battery wire to the free terminal of lamp holder B for 2 to 3 seconds. Observe the lamps.

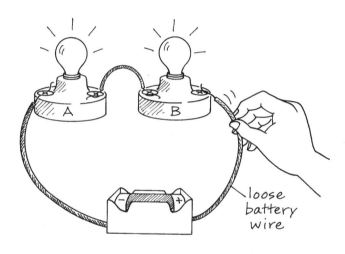

loose battery wire

6. Unscrew and remove one of the lamps and repeat step 5. Again observe the lamps.

Results

The lamps glow only when both lamps are in place and the loose battery wire is connected to lamp holder B's terminal.

Why?

The loose battery wire acts like a **switch** (a device that is used to close and open a circuit) that turns the lamps on and off. When the switch is on, the wire touches the terminal, creating a **closed circuit** (an unbroken circuit), and an electric current can flow through the wires and the lamps, thus causing the lamps to glow. When the switch is off, the wire is

removed from the terminal creating an **open circuit** (a circuit with a break in it so that no current can flow). Thus the current cannot flow, and the lamps do not glow. When a lamp is removed, this creates the same effect: the circuit is opened so that electric current cannot flow.

MORE FUN WITH CIRCUITS!

In a parallel circuit, each lamp is in its own circuit. So when one lamp is removed, the electricity can still flow through any other lamps in the parallel circuit, and they stay lit. Make a parallel circuit by preparing a second 6-inch (15-cm) wire, as in step 2 of the original experiment. Following the diagram shown, use this wire to connect the lamps in a parallel circuit. Repeat steps 5 and 6 of the original experiment.

BOOK LIST

Egan, Louise. *Thomas Edison: The Great American Inventor.* Hauppauge, N.Y.: Barron's Educational Series, Inc., 1987. Examines the life and the achievements of the famous inventor, from his boyhood experiments to his search for the incandescent lamp.

Guthridge, Sue. *Thomas A. Edison.* New York: Aladdin Paperbacks, 1959. A biography of Edison.

The Thomas Alva Edison Foundation. *The Thomas Edison Book of Easy and Incredible Experiments.* New York: Wiley, 1988. Biographical information about Edison and experiments about electricity topics.

VanCleave, Janice. *Electricity.* New York: Wiley, 1994. Experiments about circuits and other electricity topics. Each chapter contains ideas that can be turned into award-winning science fair projects.

13

Albert Einstein

Albert Einstein (1879–1955) was born in the small town of Ulm in south Germany, the first child of Hermann and Pauline Einstein. The Einsteins moved to Munich in 1880, and it was here that Hermann and his brother Jacob, who lived with the Einsteins, started a business that manufactured electric machinery. So Albert, from his early days, became acquainted with what was then the very new

electrical industry. Albert's sister Maria, called Maja, was born in 1881.

Albert had a normal childhood, although it is said that he did not talk until the age of three. Even as a young child he was a slow speaker, pausing to think about what he wanted to say. Albert's mother was an excellent pianist, and she taught Albert the violin when he was a young boy. Albert's interest in practicing increased when his mother related music to mathematics. At home, Albert was always asking his parents and his uncle Jacob questions about things that puzzled him. But at school, students were not allowed to ask questions. Instead, they learned mainly by repeating what they were told. Albert disliked school and was often bored, but he was too curious about things to let the school environment stop his learning. It was customary for families that could afford it to periodically invite college students to their homes for meals. The Einsteins invited Max Talmey, a medical student, to dine with them. They satisfied Max's hunger for food, and Max fed Albert's appetite for knowledge. Max started bringing books about science for Albert to read, and Albert became especially interested in physics and mathematics. Albert was able to understand books that were far more complicated than those he used in school. By the time he was 12, Albert's mathematical abilities were greater than those of his parents, or his uncle Jacob, or Max, so Albert had to teach himself.

In 1894, the Einsteins' family electrical business failed, and they left Germany to start another business in Milan, Italy. All of them but Albert, that is. His parents thought it best for Albert to remain in Munich with friends so that he could complete his education. Albert was very unhappy. He changed from a quiet student to the class clown. He pretended to be sick and described symptoms to his doctor that made it sound as if he was having a nervous breakdown. His doctor wrote a note to Albert's principal, suggesting that Albert join his family for a rest. Albert's principal read the note and told Albert that the school had already decided to expel him because he was a troublemaker.

Albert was 16 and unhappy about being expelled from school but happy to be reunited with his family. In Italy, Albert joined his father and uncle in their electrical business, but he wasn't interested in making electrical equipment. Instead, Albert wanted to know more about how electricity and magnetism were created. It was decided that he would go to the university and study, but he had to have a certificate of graduation from high school to enter a university. He attended a high school in Aarau, Switzerland, which was very different from the one he had attended in Germany. For the first time, Albert liked school and did well. At the end of one year he graduated and went on to the university, where again his attitude made him one of the least-loved students. He rarely attended classes because he found the lectures boring; instead he spent most of his time reading about current advances in physics and mathematics, as well as playing his violin.

Albert did have one close friend, Marcel Grossman, who faithfully attended classes and took notes. At the end of four years, each student had to take an exam. Albert had not attended very many classes during this time, so for one month before the exam, Albert studied the notes that Marcel had taken in every class. In 1900, Albert passed his exams and graduated from college.

But it was not enough to have graduated; to get a job in teaching, a person needed a recommendation from a college professor. Not one professor would write a recommendation for Einstein, so he was not able to find work teaching. He had to return to his family in Italy—basically, a failure. After months of unemployment, Albert once again received help from his friend Marcel, who found a job for him. He worked not as a professor but at the Swiss patent office in the city of Bern, where he would record the inventions of others. In 1902, Einstein started his job in the patent office, and in 1903, he married Mileva Maritsch, who had been his classmate at the university. They had two sons, Hans Albert (1904–1973), who became a successful hydraulic engineer, and Eduard (1910–1965), who had schizophrenia. A daughter, Lieserl (1902–?), was born before the marriage and is believed to have been put up for adoption. Her fate is unknown. Einstein and Mileva separated in 1914 and divorced in 1919, the same year that he married his cousin Elsa Lowenthal (1876–1936).

The patent job was perfect for Einstein. He could quickly do his work and then focus on what really interested him, such as thinking about the how and why of things, especially light.

In 1905, Einstein published three outstanding papers in a well-known German physics journal, *Annalen der Physik.* Some of his ideas shocked the scientific world and changed the way they viewed the universe. The first paper was about the photoelectric effect and stated that when light strikes the surface of a metal, it may knock off electrons from the metal. Einstein explained this by assuming that light comes in tiny energy packets, which were later called **photons,** that have both wave and particle properties. The photons, acting like particles, cause the electrons to be knocked off the metal. At first, few physicists accepted his ideas, but later they were accepted. In 1921, Einstein received a Nobel Prize for his ideas about the photoelectric effect.

The second paper was on his special theory of relativity, which is based on the idea that everything in the universe is in motion. Relative motion compares the motion of one body to the motion of another. Einstein's idea was that only light is an absolute measurement and has the same speed regardless of the position of the observer. The third paper was on a mathematical theory of the motion of molecules.

Later, in 1905, Einstein compared the relationship between mass and energy. Einstein said that under extraordinary conditions, mass can be converted into energy and energy into mass. He introduced what became perhaps the world's most famous equation: $E = mc^2$. This equation explains the relationship between mass and energy and reads: energy is equal to the product of mass times the square of the speed of light (186,000 miles per second [300,000 km per second]).

With his publications, Einstein assumed that he could gain a higher degree in physics and a teaching position at a university in Bern. But he was told that he would have to write another paper. He was angry at first but later wrote the necessary paper. In 1908, he was awarded his degree and permission to teach physics part-time. With only four students in his first class, he continued to work at the patent office.

In 1917, Einstein published his general theory of relativity, which extended his first theory to include objects that are accelerated (that change speed). In this paper, Einstein described the space around an object as being distorted, which produces an acceleration in objects passing by. He visualized space as being like a stretched elastic sheet, in which heavy objects, such as the Sun, cause an indentation. This indentation affects the paths of objects moving nearby. For centuries scientists had believed that light traveled in a straight line, but Einstein said that light bends as it travels through space. In 1919, during a total eclipse, scientists took pictures of the light emitted from the stars that were located near the Sun, and the light bent almost as much as Einstein had predicted. After this, the whole world became more interested in what he had to say.

Albert Einstein became one of the most recognized scientists in history. He received honorary doctorate degrees in science, medicine, and philosophy from many European and American universities. During the 1920s, he lectured in Europe, America, and the Far East and received many awards. In 1932, he became a professor at Princeton University in the United States. He planned to divide his time between the United States and his home in Berlin. But

Einstein was Jewish, and in 1933, Adolf Hitler came to power in Germany. Because Hitler hated Jews, Einstein remained in the United States and became a citizen in 1940.

In 1939, at the start of the Second World War, Einstein wrote to President Roosevelt that scientists in Germany were exploring nuclear reactions. He explained that this knowledge could lead to the construction of a new type of bomb that would be more powerful than any previously made. Even though Einstein was an advocate of peace, for the safety of the world, he urged the United States to discover this reaction before Germany did. It was Einstein's letter that led President Roosevelt to fund research for developing this weapon, called an atomic bomb. In 1941, the United States started the Manhattan Project, the scientific and military program that would build the atomic bomb. Einstein was denied security clearance to work on the project because he was known to be an advocate of peace. Scientists working on the atomic bomb were not allowed to even consult with Einstein because he was considered a security risk. In 1945, atomic bombs were dropped on two Japanese cities, Hiroshima and Nagasaki, hastening the end of the Second World War.

While Einstein's equation $E = mc^2$ explains the energy released in an atomic bomb, it doesn't explain how to build one. His only role in regard to the bomb was warning President Roosevelt. He came to regret taking even this step. He has been quoted as saying that if he had known that the Germans would not succeed in developing an atomic bomb, he would have done nothing. One week before his death, Einstein gave permission for his name to go on a document urging all nations to give up nuclear weapons. The man who is incorrectly given credit for the atomic bomb was actually a man who promoted international peace.

In 1952, Einstein was asked to become president of Israel. He declined.

Einstein died on April 18, 1955, in Princeton, New Jersey. He was cremated, and his ashes were scattered at an undisclosed location.

FUN TIME!

Purpose

To model the path of an object in warped space.

Materials

drawing compass
14-by-14-inch (35-by-35-cm) piece of poster board
scissors
transparent tape
bowl with a diameter of 5 to 7 inches (12.5 to 17.5 cm)
towel
sheet of copy paper
marble

Procedure

1. Use the compass to draw a circle with a 12-inch (30-cm) diameter on the poster board.

2. With the scissors, cut out the circle, then cut a line from the edge of the circle to its center.

3. Overlap the circle by about 1 inch (2.5 cm) at the edge to form a cone. Secure the cone with tape.

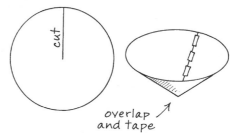

4. Turn the cone over and center it in the bowl. Secure the bowl to the cone with tape.

5. Lay the towel on a table. (The towel will help prevent the marble from rolling off the table.)

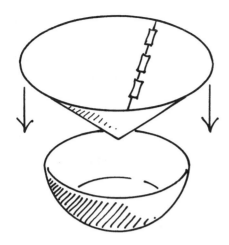

6. Roll the sheet of paper into a tube large enough for the marble to easily roll through. Secure the paper with tape.

7. Set the bowl on one end of the towel, with the attached cone facing up.

8. Place one end of the paper tube on the edge of the cone. Raise the tube slightly and allow the marble to roll through the tube and onto the cone. Observe the path of the marble on the cone. Make note of where the marble starts, and if it exits, note the position.

9. Repeat step 8 several times, increasing the amount the tube is raised each time.

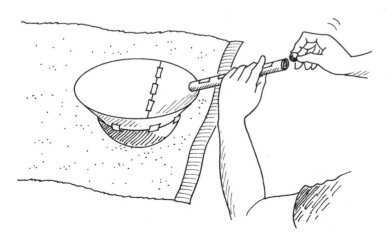

Results

With the height of the end of the tube at its lowest, the path of the marble is more curved. As the height of the tube increases, the speed of the marble increases and its path is straighter.

Why?

Mass measures the amount of matter a substance has; the more matter, the more mass. Mass also determines the gravity of an object; the more mass, the more gravity. Einstein visualized gravity as warped space. In other words, warped space is like an elastic sheet with celestial bodies on it. Each body causes the sheet to sink in. The more massive the body, the greater the indentation, thus the greater the gravity of the body. The path of moving objects in space is affected by warped (indented) space. The greater the indention, the greater the gravity; thus the more curved will be the object's path. The speed of the object also affects its path. The faster the object, the straighter will be its path. The cone in this experiment models warped space, and the moving marble models an object passing by. When a relatively slowly moving celestial body, represented by the slower moving marble, passes near an area where space is warped, the body follows a more curved path. For example, a ball thrown into the air follows a curved space created by Earth's gravity. Planets orbit the Sun for the same reason; they follow the curved space created by the Sun's gravity. Faster moving bodies follow an open curved path, and very fast bodies are only slightly deflected.

MORE FUN WITH LIGHT!

Einstein's theory that light from a star would be slightly deflected when passing by the Sun was confirmed in 1919, when the Sun was

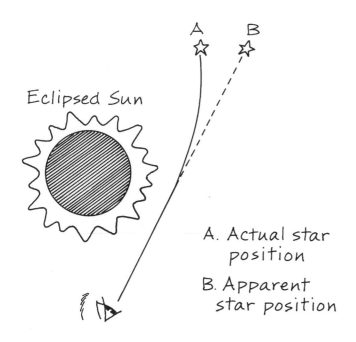

Eclipsed Sun

A B

A. Actual star position

B. Apparent star position

that you cannot see through. Stick a penny in the center of the clay, then place the bowl near the edge of a table. Stand near the table so that you can see the entire coin. Slowly move backward until the coin is just barely out of sight. Continue to look toward the bowl as a helper slowly fills it with water. The coin again becomes visible and appears to be in a different place. The light is refracted, which is a change in the direction of light caused by its moving from one substance to another. In this experiment, light from the coin refracts when it moves from the water into the air. Although this is different from the deflection due to warped space, the apparent shift in the position of an object due to a change in the direction of light is the same.

eclipsed in a part of the sky where there were a number of bright stars. The light from the stars was slightly deflected when it passed by the Sun, thus giving the impression that the position of the stars had changed.

You can alter the path of light and observe how the position of an object can appear to change. Do this by placing a walnut-size clay ball into the center of a small bowl

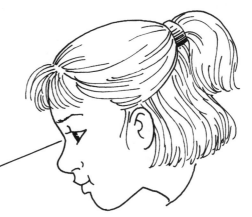

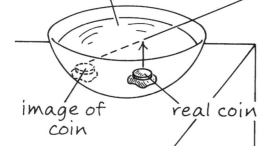

water

image of coin

real coin

BOOK LIST

Cwiklik, Robert. *Albert Einstein and the Theory of Relativity.* Hauppauge, N.Y.: Barrons, 1987. A biography of Albert Einstein.

Hammontree, Marie. *Albert Einstein.* New York: Aladdin Paperbacks, 1964. A biography of Albert Einstein.

VanCleave, Janice. *Physics for Every Kid.* New York: Wiley, 1991. Fun, simple physics experiments, including information about gravity.

Alexander Fleming

Alexander Fleming (1881–1955) was born on a farm in Darvel, Scotland, in 1881. He and his seven brothers and sisters spent much of their time playing in the streams and the country-side near their home, which was a mile from the nearest neighbor. Fleming later said that this was a time in which he unconsciously learned a great deal about nature and developed his keen sense of observation.

Fleming had to walk several miles to school. On cold days, his mother gave him freshly baked potatoes for lunch. The potatoes served two purposes: when carried in his pockets, they could keep his hands warm and, of course, he later ate them. At 13, after his father died, Fleming decided to join his older brother in London, in order to continue his education. But in a short time he had to quit school, due to lack of money.

In 1900, Fleming joined the London

Scottish Rifle Volunteers. He did not have to go to war, but he learned to be a very good shot with a rifle and played on the group's water polo team. Oddly enough, both of these experiences influenced the direction of his life. At some point he received enough money to enter medical school (some say that he received a small inheritance from his uncle). There were twelve medical schools in London to choose from. Three of the schools were equidistant from his home, one being St. Mary's. He had no knowledge of any of the schools, except that he had once played water polo against St. Mary's, so St. Mary's Hospital Medical School was his choice.

In 1906, Fleming graduated from medical school and was offered a job as a microbiologist by Sir Almroth Wright, chief of the St. Mary's bacteriology laboratory. **Bacteriology** is the study of **bacteria** (a type of microorganism). At Wright's laboratory, scientists were working to learn more about bacteria so that more vaccines could be discovered. A **vaccine** is a substance containing dead, weakened, or living microorganisms that can be injected into the body or taken orally in order to cause the body to produce **antibodies** (chemicals in the body that help protect it from a disease caused by a specific organism). (In 1769, the British physician Edward Jenner [1749–1823] discovered the first vaccine. It was used against smallpox.) Wright offered Fleming the job, not because of his outstanding academic record but because he was skilled with a rifle. It seems that St. Mary's Hospital had a good rifle team and wanted Fleming to be on it. He took the job and started a career that led to one of the most famous medical discoveries of all time.

When asked about his work, Fleming used to say, "I play with microbes." Fleming loved to grow microbes that formed pictures. Once he grew brightly colored microbes in the design and colors of the Union Jack (the British flag)

for the visiting queen of England. It took a great deal of knowledge about microbes to accomplish this, but the queen was not impressed.

In 1914, World War I began in Europe, and Fleming served with distinction in the Royal Army Medical Corps in France. He discovered that the **antiseptic** (a substance used to kill or prevent the growth of germs on the skin's surface) being used to treat soldiers' wounds was too strong and often killed **white blood cells** (the part of blood that fights germs) faster than it killed germs. Since white blood cells are the body's defense against germs, strong antiseptics caused more harm than good. Fleming suggested that doctors clean the wounds with a mixture of salt and water and cover them with a sterile bandage, instead of using the harsh antiseptic. Few doctors accepted this advice, and little was done to relieve the suffering of many soldiers. So Fleming's later work grew out of his interest in better antiseptics.

In 1915, while on leave from his war work in France, Fleming married Sarah McElroy, a nurse. Sarah and Alexander Fleming were very different. He liked to relax and talked very little; she was always busy and very talkative. Their only child, Robert, was born in 1925.

In 1918, Fleming returned to his research work at St. Mary's, and in 1921, he accidentally discovered that a chemical in his own tears killed a bacteria he was growing. He had a cold and was growing germs from his own nasal liquid. A tear fell from his eye onto the growing bacteria. Later he observed a clear space where the tear fell. He correctly concluded that the tear contained a natural antiseptic that destroyed the bacteria it had touched. Since the tear came from his eye, he concluded that the substance in the tear was not harmful to human tissue. He named the substance **lysozyme** (an antiseptic found in body fluids). To test the effects of lysozyme, Fleming needed a supply of teardrops. So, he put drops of lemon juice in his eyes to encourage the flow of tears (not a very safe procedure because the acid in lemon juice can damage the eye).

The germs that lysozyme killed were relatively harmless, but Fleming's lysozyme work increased his interest in **antibacterial** (destructive to the growth of bacteria) substances. In 1928, while he was seeking a substance to kill the bacterium staphylococcus, another accident occurred. As before, an unexpected substance entered the dish containing his bacterial growth. This time it was a mold, which Fleming later identified as *Penicillium notatum*. Usually, a contaminated experiment is thrown away, but Fleming turned this ruined experiment into one of the greatest medical advances in history. He has been quoted as saying that if it had not been for the discovery of lysozyme, he might have discarded the dish contaminated with mold, assuming that the bacterial growth had been ruined by the mold. Instead, he made a close examination and discovered that around the green mold was a clear area. Something from the mold had killed the bacteria. He kept the mold alive and began doing more tests with it. In 1929, he published a report stating that the mold produced a substance that he called penicillin, which was a powerful microbe killer that did not injure human tissue.

Fleming's discovery was largely ignored until 1938, when the Oxford University scientists Ernst Boris Chain (1906–1979) and Howard Walter Florey (1898–1968) remembered Fleming's work with mold. Florey and Chain developed penicillin into a useful antibiotic by 1941. World War II interfered with the production of penicillin in Great Britian, but methods for its mass production were developed in the United States. American scientists also tried to find a mold that would produce more penicillin and tested different molds from all around the world. In 1943, Mary Hunt, a laboratory worker, brought in an ordinary supermarket cantaloupe infected with a mold. This golden-colored mold more than doubled the amount of penicillin produced. Thousands of lives have been saved by penicillin since its discovery.

In 1945, Fleming, Chain, and Florey shared the Nobel Prize in medicine for the discovery and perfection of penicillin. Fleming's wife, Sarah, died in 1949, and in 1953, Fleming married a Greek research bacteriologist, Amalia Coutsouris. In 1957, penicillin was first **synthesized** (man-made) in the laboratory, and in 1960, **semisynthetic penicillins** (part mold, part synthetic) were made.

FUN TIME!

Purpose

To determine how the antiseptic hydrogen peroxide works.

Materials

two 10-ounce (300-mL) clear plastic glasses
3% hydrogen peroxide
cold tap water
2 slices of raw potato
clock or watch

Procedure

1. Fill one of the plastic glasses ¼ full with hydrogen peroxide.

2. Fill the remaining plastic glass ¼ full with water.

3. Place a potato slice in each of the glasses.

4. Observe the potato slices in each glass periodically for 5 or more minutes.

potato and water   potato and hydrogen peroxide

Results

Bubbles of gas are seen on the potato and rising to the surface in the glass of hydrogen peroxide. Few to no bubbles are seen in the glass of water.

Why?

Any bubbles in the glass of water are air bubbles. The effervescence (bubbling) in the glass of hydrogen peroxide is due to the presence of oxygen gas, which is produced by the **decomposition** (breaking into small parts) of the hydrogen peroxide. Cutting the potato breaks some of the plant's **cells** (building blocks of organisms), releasing chemicals, including catalase. **Catalase** is an **enzyme** (a chemical that changes the speed of chemical reactions in cells). Hydrogen peroxide is effective against bacteria, but when hydrogen peroxide comes in contact with catalase, the hydrogen peroxide decomposes, forming oxygen and water.

The oxygen and water cause effervescence that cleans the wound but are not very effective against bacteria. Thus, hydrogen peroxide is an antiseptic but is best used for washing out cuts and scrapes.

MORE FUN WITH HYDROGEN PEROXIDE!

Dirt is a common name for **soil,** which is composed of particles from rock mixed with **humus** (the material formed by decomposed organisms). Since catalase is found in most organisms, dirt contains catalase. See for yourself that dirt in a wound causes hydrogen peroxide to effervesce. Do this by putting 1 teaspoon (5 mL) of dirt in a 10-ounce (300-mL) clear plastic glass. Slightly tilt the glass and pour in ¼ cup (63 ml) of hydrogen peroxide. Let the liquid flow down the inside of the glass so that it mixes slowly with the dirt. Set the glass upright and observe its contents periodically for 5 or more minutes. Observe the color of the foam that forms on the top.

dirty foam
dirt

BOOK LIST

Gottfried, Ted. *Alexander Fleming: Discoverer of Penicillin.* New York: Scholastic, 1997. A biography of Fleming, focusing on his discovery of penicillin.
VanCleave, Janice. *The Human Body for Every Kid.* New York: Wiley, 1995. Facts and fun, simple experiments about the human body.

15

Benjamin Franklin

Benjamin Franklin (1706–1790) was born in Boston, Massachusetts. His father, Josiah Franklin, a candle maker by trade, had seventeen children, and Benjamin was his fifteenth child. Ben's mother, Abiah Folger, was his father's second wife and the mother of ten of his children. Ben taught himself to read and could read books when he was five.

The Franklins had a modest income, enough to take care of the family but not enough to send their children to school. Not many children went to school during the **era** (a period of time in history) when Ben was growing up, especially the children of tradesmen like his father. Even at the free public schools, parents had to buy books and pay a share of the cost of the firewood burned. But Ben's parents wanted their children to be educated, so on special occasions, guests, such as teachers or traveling businessmen, were invited for dinner. The guests didn't know they had been invited to teach the Franklin children. Mr.

Franklin would ask questions about the guests' travels or books they had read and anything that he thought might be worthwhile for his children to learn. Ben was more attentive to what these guests had to say than were the other Franklin children. The Franklins realized that Ben was an exceptional student, so when Ben's father received a special order for candles, the Franklins used the money to send Ben to school. He excelled in all of his classes except mathematics. This may have been due to the fact that his teacher would not allow him to ask questions, and he had no books that explained what to do. He later bought a mathematics book and became very skilled at math. Ben loved school, but after only two years, at the age of 10, he was taken out of school because the Franklins could no longer afford it.

From early childhood, Ben was a thinker and a problem solver. Even when playing as a child, he thought of ways to solve problems. For example, when he was about 10 years old, he wanted to swim faster, so he invented a type of flipper for his feet that increased his swimming speed. He was well-known around town for his experimenting. One day word got out that he was going to try an experiment at the pond, and many of the children in his neighborhood gathered to watch. Ben was going to use a kite to pull him across the widest part of the pond. It was a successful adventure, but since the wind was blowing in only one direction, Ben had to walk a long way back around the pond. Still, his "swimming kite" was the talk of the town.

Ben played and experimented as often as possible, but he also had to help his father make candles and soap. His father knew that Ben was unhappy in this job, and he feared that Ben, like one of his older brothers, would run off to sea. When Ben was 12, Mr. Franklin decided that Ben should be an apprentice for his brother James, who had a print shop. Ben didn't want to do this but agreed to please his parents. He had to sign a contract legally binding him to work for James until he was 21 years old. As an apprentice, he would be taught the print business, and his brother would house, feed, and clothe him, but Ben would not be paid.

Ben liked his job at first because he loved to read. He quickly read the few books that his brother had and was lucky to make friends with a boy who was an apprentice in a bookseller's shop. Ben was able to borrow books each night, as long as he returned them early the next morning. But since he worked long hours, he had no time to sleep if he read the books. He came up with a plan that would allow him to have money to buy books. Ben's idea was that if James would give him half the money that his food cost, he would buy his own food. James agreed, and from then on Ben ate very little, in order to have money for books. Since it didn't take him long to eat his lunch, he had most of the hour to read.

Ben's brother James was not always kind to him, and in 1723, at the age of 17, Ben quarreled with James and ran away to Philadelphia, Pennsylvania. He found jobs to support himself and in 1728 opened his own print shop. In 1729, he began publishing a highly successful newspaper called the *Pennsylvania Gazette*. In 1730, Ben married Deborah Read, and they had three children: two sons, William and Francis, and one daughter, Sarah.

Ben Franklin was successful not only in business but also in public service. He started the first public library in 1731 and organized the first volunteer fire department in 1736. He also developed many successful inventions, such as the Franklin stove. The stove, a metal box in which wood was burned, provided more heat with less wood than was required by the open fires usually used to heat homes. Soon people in every American colony, as well as in Europe—even kings—had a Franklin stove. Franklin was such a successful businessman that he was able to retire at the age of 42. He said that he was going to read, think, study, and talk with worthy men about things that would benefit mankind. He may have retired from his regular business routine, but he didn't retire from learning, creating, and being politically active. He was an important figure in the American Revolution and was in fact the only one of the Founding Fathers to sign all four of the major documents that made the United States of America possible: the Declaration of Independence, the Wartime Treaty with France, the Peace Treaty with England, and the Constitution of the United States of America.

Franklin was fascinated with all forms of science but especially with electricity. Electricity was a great mystery in Franklin's day, and static electricity experiments were often used at adult parties as part of the entertainment. Some people thought that electricity was magic, but Franklin believed it to be a force of nature. The term *battery* was coined by Franklin to refer to a Leyden jar (a device used to store static electricity). However, the first workable device for generating a consistent flow of electricity, a battery, was invented around 1799 by the Italian inventor Alessandro Volta. Volta's discovery formed the basis for nearly all modern batteries. Other electrical terms coined by Franklin include *charged, electrician, plus and minus,* and *positive and negative.*

Ben Franklin is best known for another kite experiment. Along with a few other scientists of his day, Franklin believed that lightning and electricity were the same thing. In 1752, Franklin designed an experiment to prove that his idea was right. Pictures of this famous experiment often show Franklin with a young boy as they stand outside flying a kite, with lightning flashing in the sky (such as on page 22). This is most unlikely, since Franklin was well aware of the dangers of electricity. Instead, some accounts of the event say that with the help of his son William, who was 22 at

the time, Franklin flew the kite when the storm clouds first appeared but before lightning was seen. Instead of being outdoors, he was inside a building. He hoped to draw electricity out of the storm clouds. He had already discovered that metals with points attracted electricity, and a Leyden jar could be used to collect the electricity. So he attached a sharp pointed wire to the top of the kite to attract the electricity in the clouds. A key was attached at the bottom of the kite string, and a silk ribbon was attached to the key. A Leyden jar was attached to the key by a metal wire to collect the electricity. Franklin held onto the dry silk ribbon, which acted as an **electrical insulator** (a material that does not easily allow electricity to flow through it). Being inside a building kept the silk ribbon dry, which was important since electricity would have been able to flow through the wet material.

Thankfully, lightning did not actually strike Franklin's kite, or he and William might have been killed. At first, Franklin thought that the experiment was a failure. But then he saw some of the tiny fibers on the string standing out, and when he reached toward the key, a bright blue electric spark jumped from the key to his hand. During a thunderstorm, violent air currents move up and down inside clouds, rubbing water droplets and ice crystals against each other. This movement is but one of the processes that fills clouds with a charge of static electricity. Some of the charges collected on the string and the key and in the Leyden jar of Franklin's experiment. Like the blue spark, lightning is an **electric discharge** (a loss of static electricity).

Franklin put the information he learned from the kite experiment to use by designing lightning rods for homes. His lightning rod was a pointed metal rod on the top of a house, which was attached to a wire that led to the ground. Lightning was attracted to the rod and ran down the wire to the ground, instead of hitting the house and setting it on fire. Not only had Franklin plucked lightning out of the sky, he had figured out a way to control it and help people at the same time.

Franklin also made some of the earliest studies of surface currents in the ocean. He studied the Gulf Stream, which is a surface current off the eastern coast of North America. Franklin found that the temperature of the water could be used to determine the boundary of the current. Ocean currents like the Gulf Stream can be used by sailors to increase a ship's speed, so it was important for sailors to know where the currents were.

FUN TIME!

Purpose

To model how clouds produce static electricity.

Materials

sheet of white copy paper
salt shaker with salt
transparent tape dispenser

Procedure

1. Lay the paper on a table.

2. Sprinkle a thin layer of salt over most of the paper.

3. Pull off about 8 inches (20 cm) of tape from the tape dispenser. Do not let the tape touch anything.

4. Hold the ends of the tape, one end in each hand, with the nonsticky side facing down.

5. Pull the tape tight and slowly lower it toward the salt-covered paper until the salt moves toward the tape.

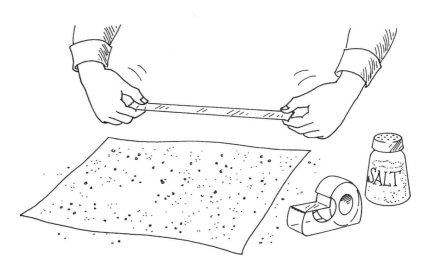

Results

The particles of salt jump up and stick to the nonsticky side of the tape.

Why?

When particles in clouds rub against each other, some of the atoms of the cloud particles are pulled apart. This is much like the atoms in the tape of this experiment, which are pulled apart when you pull the tape off the dispenser. Usually, an atom has the same number of electrons (negative charges) as protons (positive charges). When the cloud particles rub together, electrons are lost by some particles and gained by others. Likewise, when the tape is unrolled, the sticky and the nonsticky sides separate; electrons are lost by one side and gained by the other side. If the sticky side gains electrons, it will be negatively charged, and if the nonsticky side loses electrons, it will be positively charged. Whether it is cloud particles or pieces of tape, a buildup of charges results in the material having static electricity.

Like charges **repel** (push apart) and unlike charges **attract** (pull together). So, assuming the nonsticky side is positively charged, when you hold the positively charged strip over the salt, the negatively charged electrons in the surface of the salt facing the tape strip are attracted to the tape. When some of the electrons move toward an area, the area then has more electrons than protons. Thus the surface of the salt facing the charged tape has more electrons, giving it a negative charge. This is called **charging by induction** (the process of charging a neutral material by holding a charged object near but not touching it). Because there is a buildup of negative charges on the salt's surface facing the tape, the salt particles have static electricity. The positively charged tape attracts the negatively charged salt, and the salt jumps up to the tape. The salt sticks to the tape due to the attraction between the unlike charges—the positively charged tape and the negatively charged salt.

As a result of charging by induction, the negative charges in clouds cause a positive charge on the ground below. When this charge is great enough, there is an electrical discharge, with the negative charges in the cloud moving toward the ground. This is how lightning is formed. Some lightning is an electrical discharge between two clouds.

MORE FUN WITH CHARGES!

The salt and the tape attract each other because they have unlike charges. See how materials with like charges repel each other. Do this by using two pieces of tape. First, place a book near the edge of table. Place about half of a ruler under the book, with the other part of the ruler extending past the edge of the table. Pull off about 8 inches (20 cm) of tape from the tape dispenser. Secure one end of the tape to the end of the ruler so that the tape hangs from the ruler. Pull off

another 8-inch (20-cm) piece of tape. Hold the ends of the tape, one end in each hand. Stretch the tape tight,and hold the sticky side near but not touching the hanging tape. Notice the movement of the hanging tape. Repeat, turning the tape in your hands so that the non-sticky side is facing the hanging tape.

BOOK LIST

Davidson, Margaret. *The Story of Benjamin Franklin.* New York: Bantam Doubleday, 1988. A biography of Benjamin Franklin.

Franklin Institute Science Museum. *Ben Franklin Book of Easy & Incredible Experiments.* New York: Wiley, 1995. A book of activities, projects, and science fun about subjects that especially interested Benjamin Franklin.

Stevenson, Augusta. *Benjamin Franklin.* New York: Aladdin, 1983. A biography of Benjamin Franklin.

VanCleave, Janice. *Electricity.* New York: Wiley, 1994. Experiments with static electricity and other electricity topics. Each chapter contains ideas that can be turned into award-winning science fair projects.

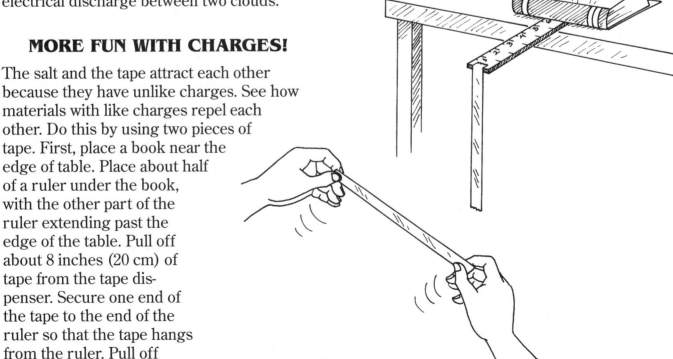

16

Galileo Galilei

The Italian scientist Galileo Galilei (1564–1642) was the oldest of seven children born to Vincenzo Galilei and Giulia Ammanati. His parents wanted Galileo to study medicine because they believed it to be a career that would provide him with a good income. So, he entered the University of Pisa in 1581 to study medicine. But Galileo soon realized that he was more interested in mathematics and in figuring out how things behaved, such as how celestial bodies move and how quickly different objects fall.

Galileo was one of the pioneers of the experimental approach to science, which involves making observations, asking questions, making **hypotheses** (guesses, based on facts, about the answer to a question), and experimenting to find the answers. Unlike Aristotle and other great philosophers, Galileo believed that an idea had to be proved in order to be accepted. Galileo's work was first recorded in a biography written by one of his students, Vincenzo Viviani (1622–1703). It is thought that many of the stories about how Galileo performed some of his experiments may have been slight exaggerations by Viviani. But however he did it, Galileo discovered many scientific truths.

Viviani describes one of Galileo's most famous experiments, a swinging lamp, as occurring in the Cathedral at Pisa in Italy around 1582. While in the cathedral, Galileo became curious about a lamp that was swinging back and forth from a chain attached to the ceiling. Galileo noticed that no matter how big the **arc** (the portion of a circle) traced by the swing of the lamp, each swing seemed to take the same amount of time. Watches did not exist in that era, so he used his own pulse to compare the timing of each swing. He was correct; the timing of each swing was the same, no matter what the size of the arc. This observation provided information that eventually led to the invention of the pendulum clock in 1656 by Christiaan Huygens (1629–1695).

In 1586, at 22, Galileo had lost all interest in studying medicine, and his father no longer had the money to pay for his schooling. So Galileo withdrew from the University of Pisa without a degree and returned home to live with his family. He continued to study science and mathematics on his own. In 1589, with the help of influential friends, Galileo was given a three-year position as a professor of mathematics at the University of Pisa, even though he had not graduated from the university.

At this time, Galileo is said to have made his famous experiments from the Leaning Tower of Pisa (the freestanding bell tower of the Cathedral at Pisa). He dropped two cannonballs of different weights from the tower to show his students that falling bodies of different weights would hit the ground at the same time. His objective was to demonstrate the error of Aristotle's theory that heavy things fall faster than lighter things.

Other professors at the university were angry with Galileo for questioning Aristotle's ideas. In his lectures, Galileo made fun of these other professors for having such closed minds. Galileo became so unpopular at the school that there was talk that he might be fired. Again his friends helped him out, this time finding him a job at the University of Padua, also in Italy. But teaching was mainly just a way for Galileo to make money. His real goal was to become financially independent so he could do research and experiment. Many of Galileo's important discoveries came from attempts to impress influential people, who he hoped might offer him a well-paying appointment.

In 1609, Galileo first heard of a spy glass (telescope) that had been invented in Holland. Before this time, he had little interest in astronomy. But he was intrigued by the new device and soon built his own telescope, with which he studied the heavens. In 1610, Galileo published his findings, including the fact that the Milky Way was composed of stars and that

Jupiter had four moons, among other discoveries. He dedicated the publication to one of his former students, Cosimo, who was now the grand duke of Tuscany. He also made a beautiful telescope, which he presented as a gift to the grand duke, and he named the moons of Jupiter after the grand duke's family. Galileo did all of this in hopes that Cosimo would become his **patron** (a person who supports another, providing a salary and living expenses). His dream came true, and in 1610, the grand duke appointed Galileo his chief mathematician and philosopher, as well as a professor of mathematics at the University of Pisa.

Unfortunately, this meant that Galileo was back at the university where the professors not only disagreed with him but now were jealous of his success and determined to discredit him as well. Galileo might not have gotten in so much trouble if he had worked quietly, but he liked making his enemies mad. He was so smart that he usually won arguments, which made people even madder. His enemies were determined to bring Galileo down. Galileo was accused of making statements that contradicted (went against) the Bible, an act of heresy that could cost Galileo his life. Other scientists, including the German astronomer Johannes Kepler (1571–1630), advised Galileo not to anger his enemies. They feared that it would be dangerous for him, and they were correct.

Galileo said that he had discovered evidence supporting Copernicus's heliocentric (Sun-centered) model of the universe, which at the time was considered heresy by the Catholic Church. Galileo made things worse for himself by saying that anyone who did not support the heliocentric theory was being stubbornly stupid. This was like saying that the Pope and his advisers were stupid. In 1616, the Church declared the heliocentric theory false and commanded Galileo to stop teaching it. He had little choice but to denounce his beliefs in a "Sun-centered" universe and promise that he would never again teach it. It was a promise that he did not keep, but for a time he did not publicly announce his beliefs. It wasn't that Galileo did not support the beliefs of the Catholic Church; he just didn't agree with what, in his opinion, were rules made by men and not by God.

Galileo received permission from the Catholic Church to write a book comparing the heliocentric and geocentric (Earth-centered) models of the universe. Galileo told the Church authorities that the book would give equal representation to the two theories. In February 1632, the book, called *The Dialogue,* was published. It was written more like a story than a science book, and it became a best-seller not only in Italy but throughout Europe. But the book did not give equal representation to the two theories. Instead, it provided more support for the heliocentric theory. Galileo had defied the order of the Catholic Church and had publicly supported the heliocentric theory. But more than that, Galileo's enemies convinced the Pope that one of the characters in the book was really a caricature of the Pope and was meant to show how stupid he was. In August, an order was given to stop printing the book, and in October, Galileo was ordered to Rome to stand trial. At the time, Galileo was 68 and in very poor health. His doctor reported that traveling might kill him, but the response from the Pope was that Galileo would come or would be brought in chains.

Galileo was carried to Rome on a bed in a horse-drawn wagon. He was in danger of being killed for his actions, so he took the advice of his friends and did not argue with his accusers. He said that he had forgotten his promise of not promoting the Sun-centered theory and agreed to get on his knees and say that his idea of Earth moving around a stationary Sun was false. But some say that upon rising, he whispered quietly, "And yet it does move." He lied to save his life but spoke the truth even if he was the only one who would hear it.

Church officials ordered that all copies of Galileo's book *The Dialogue* be burned. They banned his other books in Italy, but Galileo knew that his works would continue to be published in other parts of the world. He was expecting a light sentence and was shocked to receive life in prison. Again his important friends came to the rescue, and he did not go to prison. Instead, he was sentenced to house arrest in the home of a friend in Siena. Galileo later asked that he be confined to a small farm he owned at Arcetri, which was near Florence and his favorite daughter, Sister Maria Celeste. At first he was not allowed to have visitors, but later, visitors who were approved by the Church were allowed.

Maria Celeste died about four months after Galileo arrived at Arcetri. He was very sad but soon continued his research. By 1637, after years of having problems with his eyes, most likely due to looking at the Sun through his telescope, he was totally blind. Because he was nearly helpless, the restrictions were relaxed a little, and he was allowed to have two students come and help him with his research and experiments. Galileo died on January 8, 1642, the same year that Sir Isaac Newton was born. It has been said that Galileo discovered how things moved and Newton went on to discover why. (See chapter 22 for information about Newton.)

Viviani tried to have a grand funeral for Galileo, but because he died a prisoner who had been convicted of heresy, the Church did not allow it. So a simple funeral took place, and Galileo was buried in a family cemetery. On March 12, 1737, his remains were transferred to what was considered a more fitting burial place in the Church of Santa Croce, in Florence. During this transfer of his body, someone cut off the middle finger of Galileo's right hand. The finger was acquired by Angelo M. Bandini, the librarian of the Biblioteca Laurenziana, and was exhibited for a long period in this library. The finger was placed on display to honor the great scientist who had pointed to the stars and revealed some of their mystery. Today the finger is on display in the Florence Institute and Museum of the History of Science, in Italy. In 1822, the Catholic Church lifted the ban on Galileo's books, and on October 31, 1992, the Church removed the verdict of heresy against Galileo.

FUN TIME!

Purpose

To determine the effect of mass on the acceleration of falling objects.

Material

quarter
sheet of white copy paper
pencil
scissors
small rug or towel

Procedure

1. Lay the coin on the paper and trace around the coin.

2. Cut out the tracing, cutting the circle on the inside of the marks so that the circle is slightly smaller than the coin.

3. Place the rug on the floor.

4. Stand near the edge of the rug.

5. Hold the coin in one hand and the paper circle in the other so that the flat side of each is parallel with the floor.

6. Hold your hands as high as possible in front of your body and over the rug. (The rug will prevent the coin from rolling when dropped.)

Results

When dropped separately, the coin falls faster than the paper circle. When dropped together, one on top of the other, the coin and the paper circle fall together.

Why?

Acceleration is the change in the **velocity** (the speed in a particular direction) of an object. Earth's gravity causes everything to fall at a rate called **gravitational acceleration** (a change in speed due to the force of gravity) of 32 ft/sec^2 (9.8 m/sec^2). This means that if gravity is the only force acting on a falling object, its falling speed would increase 32 ft/sec (9.8 m/sec) for every second that it falls. Thus at the end of one second the speed of the falling object would be 32 ft/sec (9.8 m/sec), at the end of two seconds its speed would be 64 ft/sec (19.6 m/sec), and so on. But since objects falling toward Earth fall through air, air pushes against falling objects and slows them down. The effect of the air on an object depends on an object's mass. This experiment shows that when falling separately, the object with the greater mass (coin) falls faster because the difference between the amount of gravity pulling it down and the upward force of the air is much greater than that of the object with lesser mass (paper circle). But when placed one on top of the other, the two objects will fall at the same rate, which will be the rate of the more massive object, the coin. It is believed that Galileo performed a comparable experiment using a rock and a leaf.

7. Release the coin and the paper circle at the same time. Determine which object falls faster.

8. Repeat steps 4 through 6, placing the paper circle beneath the coin. Make sure that no part of the paper circle extends past the edge of the coin.

9. Repeat steps 4 through 6, placing the paper circle on top of the coin. Again, make sure that no part of the paper circle extends past the edge of the coin.

MORE FUN WITH FALLING OBJECTS!

How air hits a surface also affects how it falls. An index card is more likely to fall straight

down if it is dropped with its flat side parallel to the floor. But if held with the narrow edge to the floor, the card generally leans and air hits it at an angle, causing the card to spin and flutter about. Challenge a friend to drop 10 index cards or playing cards into a bowl, one at a time, from shoulder height above the bowl. Do not give instructions on how to hold the cards, other than the height from which to drop them. When it is your turn, hold each card perfectly flat, thumb at one side, fingers at the other, and release the card. If the cards are held perfectly parallel to the floor before being dropped, they should float like parachutes into the bowl. Any

tilt of the card will cause it to flutter and miss the bowl.

BOOK LIST

Bendick, Jeanne. *Along Came Galileo.* Sandwich, Mass.: Beautiful Feet Books, 1999. A biography of Galileo.

Filkin, David. *Stephen Hawking's Universe.* New York: BasicBooks, 1997. A brief history of the universe and the scientists who revealed its secrets, including Galileo.

Ingpen, Robert. *Scientists Who Changed the World.* New York: Chelsea House, 1994. A time line of contributions of famous scientists, including Galileo.

VanCleave, Janice. *Gravity.* New York: Wiley, 1993. Experiments about falling bodies and other gravity-related topics. Each chapter contains ideas that can be turned into award-winning science fair projects.

17

Caroline and William Herschel

The German astronomers Caroline Lucretia Herschel (1750–1848) and William Herschel (1738–1822) were born in Hanover, Germany. Their father, Isaac, was a skilled musician who became a bandmaster in the German army. Having not had a formal education himself, Isaac wanted his children—four sons and two daughters—to be educated. He especially wanted them to know astronomy, mathematics, and music. Caroline and William's mother, Anna, did not share her husband's respect for education. Only reluctantly did she accept the education of her sons, and she strongly opposed education for her daughters. Instead, she felt that girls should be taught how to do household tasks.

At the age of 10, Caroline had typhus, a disease that stunted her growth; she never grew past 4 foot, 3 inches (1.28 m). Her father believed that she was not pretty enough for a man to ever want to marry her, so he informed her that she would live her life as an old maid (a woman who never marries). His prediction came true, but it was by Caroline's choice and not because of her appearance. She lived a long, productive life and had many friends and admirers.

Although Caroline's mother didn't want Caroline to be educated, her father privately encouraged her to learn and introduced her to the wonders of astronomy. One of Caroline's memories of this time was of a clear frosty night when her father pointed out several beautiful **constellations** (groups of stars that form patterns), as well as a comet that was visible. Little did either of them know that in just a few years, Caroline would be the first woman to find and report a new comet and that she would find eight new comets in her lifetime.

In 1872, at 22, Caroline moved to Bath, England, to live with her brother William. Caroline was supposed to be her brother's housekeeper, but William, a music teacher, wanted his sister to do more. William gave Caroline voice lessons and taught her mathematics as well. Although Caroline mastered many math concepts, she was never successful in learning the multiplication tables. So she kept a copy of the tables handy for easy reference.

William's hobby was astronomy, and in his spare time, he designed and built telescopes. William became a skilled telescope maker and built the largest **reflecting telescopes** (telescopes that use mirrors and **lenses**— glass or other transparent material so shaped that it refracts light passing through it) of his time. It is said that while he polished the mirror for one of these telescopes, Caroline fed him by hand so that he did not have to stop and eat.

After a while, Caroline's job changed from being William's housekeeper to being his assistant. She calculated the positions of the celestial bodies that she and her brother discovered, and she prepared the data for publication. William was interested in identifying **double stars** (stars that appear to be close together). He published three catalogs, listing more than 800 double stars.

In 1781, using one of his powerful reflecting telescopes, William discovered a planet that he named Georgium Sidus (Star of George) in honor of King George III of Great Britain. Astronomers at this time often named their discoveries after an important person, in the hope that the person would become a patron. It worked for William, because King George III gave him a modest yearly salary of 200 pounds so that he could be a full-time astronomer. Unfortunately for King George, his name didn't stick. The planet was later called Herschel, in honor of William, and then named Uranus after Oranos, a Greek mythological character thought to be the first ruler of the universe. The name Uranus was first proposed by the German astronomer Johann Elert Bode (1747–1826).

In 1786, Caroline discovered her first comet, which some described as the "first lady's comet." As a result of this discovery, King George III gave her a yearly salary of 50 pounds so that she could be a full-time assistant to William. She was the first woman to be so recognized, but she couldn't live on this small amount of money so she was still dependent on her brother for support. When her brother died in 1822, Caroline was 72 years old. She returned to Hanover to live with her younger brother Dietrich. Even though she stopped her observational astronomy career, she started cataloging every discovery that she and William had made. She sent this information to the scientific community in England, and for this work she was made an honorary member of the Royal Astronomical Society in 1835 and the Royal Irish Academy in 1838. Germany honored her as well. On her 96th birthday, she received a letter from the king of Prussia, recognizing her for her valuable service. He also gave her the Gold Medal of Science for her life's accomplishments. In 1889, a **minor planet** (an asteroid) was named Lucretia in her honor.

FUN TIME!

Purpose

To make a model of optical double stars.

Materials

walnut-size piece of clay
ruler

Procedure

1. Divide the clay into two equal parts. Form both pieces into balls.

2. Place one ball of clay at each end of the ruler.

3. Hold the ruler in your right hand at arm's length and at eye level. Point the ruler away from your face so that the clay balls are in line with each other.

4. Close your right eye and look at the balls. Slowly turn your head toward the right until the balls appear to lie side by side.

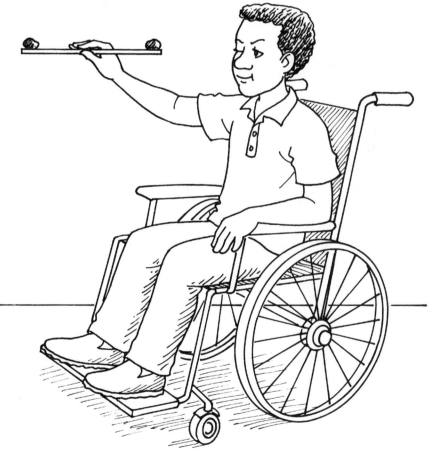

Results

The clay balls appear to be close together.

Why?

Two stars that appear to be close together are called double stars. If the stars are actually far apart and have no true relationship to each other, they are called **optical double stars.** Like the clay balls in this experiment, optical doubles appear to be close because they lie along the observer's line of sight.

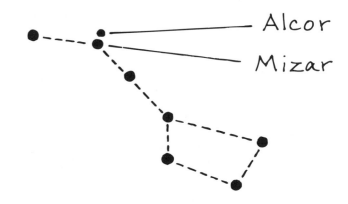

MORE FUN WITH STARS!

The Big Dipper is an **asterism** (a group of stars with a shape within a constellation) within Ursa Major (the constellation commonly called the Big Bear). The double star that includes the stars Mizar and Alcor appears to be the second star from the end of the Big Dipper's handle. According to legend, before the invention of eyeglasses, Alcor was used by some cultures as a test of one's eyesight—only people with very good vision can see it as a separate star with the naked eye. On a dark, cloudless night, face the north and find the Big Dipper. Remember that during the year, the dipper appears to rotate in a counterclockwise circle in the northern sky, and sometimes it is upside down. Look at Mizar in the dipper's handle, and see if you can see Alcor.

BOOK LIST

Hathaway, Nancy. *The Friendly Guide to the Universe.* New York: Penguin Books, 1994. Information about the universe and the scientists, including Caroline and William Herschel, who have studied it.

Osen, Lynn M. *Women in Mathematics.* Cambridge, Mass: MIT Press, 1992. The scientific achievements and obstacles of early women in science, including Caroline Herschel.

Reid, Struan, and Patricia Fara. *The Usborne Book of Scientists.* New York: Scholastic, 1992. Some of the men and women, including Caroline and William Herschel, whose discoveries have changed the world.

VanCleave, Janice. *Astronomy for Every Kid.* New York: Wiley, 1991. Fun facts and investigations about astronomy, including comets.

———. *Solar System.* New York: Wiley, 2000. Experiments about the solar system. Each chapter contains ideas that can be turned into award-winning science fair projects.

18

Antoine-Laurent Lavoisier

Antoine-Laurent Lavoisier (1743–1794) was born to Jean-Antoine Lavoisier, a lawyer of distinction, and Emilie Punctis Lavoisier, who was from a wealthy, influential family. Antoine's mother died when he was five years old, so his aunt, Constance Punctis, helped to raise him. Antoine was devoted to her. Constance saw that young Antoine had a good education, and he later attended the Collège Mazarin, where he studied a broad range of topics, including law and science. He was expected to follow in his father's footsteps and obtained his license to practice law in 1764, but his real interest was geology.

In 1768, at the young age of 25, he was elected to the Academy of Science, France's most elite scientific organization. In the same year he bought into the Farmer's General, a private company that collected taxes and tariffs for the government and whose members were allowed to keep a portion of the taxes collected. This provided Lavoisier with a source of income so that he could spend his time experimenting. It was through this company that he met Marie-Anne Pierrette Paulze, the daughter of one of its members. In 1771, he and Marie-Anne, who was not quite 14 at the time, were married.

Marie-Anne prepared herself to be her husband's scientific assistant by learning English, which Lavoisier could not speak. With a knowledge of English, she could translate the work of British chemists like Joseph Priestley (1733–1804) so that Lavoisier would know what other scientists were doing. She not only helped perform the experiments but also kept records about them and even studied art so that she could illustrate them.

Although Lavoisier began his science career as a geologist, he was most noted for chemistry, especially for discovering the role that oxygen plays in the burning of a substance, which is called **combustion** (the process of rapid combination with oxygen). His theories of combustion, his development of a new system of naming chemicals, and his writing the first modern textbook of chemistry led to his being known as the father of modern chemistry.

Many of Lavoisier's experiments involved oxygen. Joseph Priestley had just discovered that a gas he called "new air" could be produced. Lavoisier confirmed that Priestley's "new air" was a new element, and in 1778 Lavoisier suggested that the element be called *oxygen*.

Lavoisier disproved the idea that matter could be created or destroyed during a chemical reaction, such as when a substance is heated. Lavoisier heated materials in a closed container so that nothing could enter or leave and found that the weight of the container stayed the same, even though the appearance of the contents changed. He had proved that although matter changes from one form to another, the quantity of matter does not change. This is called the **law of conservation of matter.**

To make his measurements, Lavoisier invented a new scale that was accurate to 0.0005 gram. (Note that a small paper clip weighs about 1 gram. If you divided a paper clip into 10,000 parts, 0.0005 gram would equal the weight of 5 of these parts.)

Lavoisier's connection to Farmer's General eventually led to his death, when many French people became unhappy with rising and unequal taxes. Radical French revolutionaries demanded Lavoisier's life, as well as those of others involved in the tax-collecting company. On May 8, 1794, Lavoisier and all of the other members of Farmer's General were arrested, and a short trial was held. On the same day, they were all found guilty and executed. Lavoisier is said to have requested time to finish some of his experiments, but the judge had no mercy on him. Lavoisier's wife later married the scientist Count Rumford, who discredited some of Lavoisier's ideas about heat. (See chapter 24 for more information about Count Rumford.)

FUN TIME!

Purpose

To demonstrate the conservation of matter.

Materials

½ cup (125 mL) white vinegar

empty 20-ounce (600-mL) plastic soda or water bottle

1 teaspoon (5 mL) baking soda

1 sheet of bathroom tissue

9-inch (23-cm) round balloon

food scale

watch or clock

Procedure

1. Pour the vinegar into the bottle.

2. Place the baking soda in the center of the tissue.

3. Roll the tissue around the baking soda. Secure the packet by twisting the ends of the tissue.

4. Set the bottle, the packet of baking soda, and the balloon on the scale. Note the weight of the items.

5. Drop the packet of baking soda into the bottle.

6. Immediately stretch the mouth of the balloon over the bottle's mouth and allow the bottle to remain on the scale.

7. Observe the contents of the bottle and the balloon for 2 to 3 minutes.

8. At the end of the observation time, note the weight of the bottle and its contents.

Result

When the packet of baking soda and the vinegar are combined, bubbles are seen in the bottle and the balloon inflates. There are visible changes inside the bottle, but there is no change in the weight of the materials at the beginning of the experiment and the weight of the changed materials at the end of the experiment.

Why?

Baking soda consists of the chemical called sodium bicarbonate. When this chemical combines with vinegar (acetic acid), a chemical reaction occurs, producing carbon dioxide as one of the products. The gas is a visible product. Other products mix with the vinegar in the bottle and are not seen. Because you placed the balloon over the mouth of the bottle, the gas formed by the reaction could not escape. Even though the reactants broke apart and recombined in different ways, all the original parts were contained inside the bottle, thus there was no change in weight. This proves the conservation of matter that Lavoisier described.

MORE FUN WITH CHEMICALS!

There are three common **phases of matter** (forms of matter) on Earth: solid, liquid, and gas. Some chemical reactions involve **phase changes** (change in which one phase of matter changes to another), such as in the previous experiment where a gas was produced by combining a liquid and a solid. Another chemical reaction in which there is a phase change from a liquid to a solid is the combination of a **solution** (a mixture of a substance that has been dissolved in a liquid) of Epsom salts and liquid glue (Glue-All). Make this solution by thoroughly mixing together 2 teaspoons

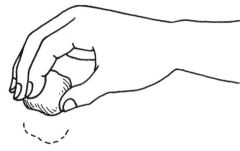

towel around the blob and squeeze the towel to press the extra liquid out of the blob. How does the blob differ from the reactants from which it was formed? Will the blob bounce? Shape the blob into a ball and drop it on a table or another flat surface to determine if it will bounce.

(10 mL) of water with 1 teaspoon (5 mL) of Epsom salts in a paper cup. (There may be a little Epsom salts that will not dissolve.) Add 1 tablespoon (15 mL) of liquid glue to the cup. Stir the contents of the cup then scoop out the solid white blob that forms, placing it on a paper towel. Fold the

BOOK LIST

Clements, Gillian. *The Picture History of Great Inventors*. New York: Knopf, 1994. Inventors from the earliest civilization to the present day, including Lavoisier.

Haven, Kendall. *Marvels of Science*. Englewood, Colo.: Libraries Unlimited, 1994. Fifty fascinating short stories about scientists, including Lavoisier.

Reid, Struan, and Patricia Fara. *The Usborne Book of Scientists*. New York: Scholastic, 1992. Some of the men and women, including Lavoisier, whose discoveries have changed the world.

VanCleave, Janice. *Chemistry for Every Kid*. New York: Wiley, 1989. Fun facts and investigations about chemistry.

Henrietta Leavitt

Henrietta Swan Leavitt (1868–1921) was born in Cambridge, Massachusetts, on the fourth of July, 1868. She was one of seven children born to George and Henrietta Leavitt. Her father was a minister and her mother a homemaker.

Leavitt had always been interested in science, but it wasn't until her last year at Radcliffe, a well-known women's college, that she took an astronomy course. She fell in love with the science, and after graduating in 1892,

she stayed at Radcliffe another year to study more about astronomy. But her astronomy studies were temporarily halted due to a serious illness. She spent two years at home recovering from this illness, which left her deaf.

In 1895, she volunteered to work at the Harvard College Observatory. Other noted women astronomers, including Annie Jump Cannon (1863–1941), worked at the observatory. Cannon, like Leavitt, was seriously hearing impaired. But neither their lack of hearing nor their sex prevented these women from pursuing their careers, even though many men objected to women being in what were considered men's jobs. Leavitt's boss, Edward Pickering, the director of the Harvard Observatory, equally encouraged the scientists working for him, whether they were men or women.

Leavitt's first job at the observatory was to be a computer! Before the age of modern electronic computers, this just meant that she computed or calculated figures. She had to compare the size of stars on two photographs taken at different times. But even though the task might have been dull to some, Leavitt liked her job and was a meticulous (very careful) worker.

In 1902, Leavitt became a permanent member of the Harvard Observatory staff and worked there until her death in 1921. Another type of research Leavitt did at the observatory involved using a **photometer** (an instrument that measures light by changing it into an electric current) to study variable stars. **Variable stars** are stars that change greatly in brightness over a period of time, some changing in only hours or days, and others requiring years. In 1912, she prepared a table comparing the changing time and the **apparent magnitude** (a measure of how bright a star appears) of variable stars. She found several thousand variable stars, about half of the known variable stars at that time. The information that she discovered about these stars paved the way for other scientists to calculate the true brightness of other stars and to determine distances of stars.

Leavitt's main research interest was using photographic photometry to determine the brightness or the magnitude of a star from a photographic image. Leavitt spent most of her life studying the magnitudes and the colors of stars. Her method for determining star color is still used today.

Although she made many major contributions to the field of astronomy, she received few honors in her lifetime. Yet she had never set out to achieve fame and glory. Leavitt is said to have cared little for personal amusement. She never married, but she was devoted to her family and her church. She died of cancer at the age of 52.

FUN TIME!

Purpose

To model a type of variable star.

Materials

2 index cards
pencil
ruler
scissors
flashlight
transparent tape
sheet of white copy paper

Procedure

1. Lay the index cards together and fold them in half by placing their short sides together.

2. Using the pencil and ruler, draw a semicircle with about a 1-inch (2.5-cm) diameter on the folded edges of the cards.

3. Using the scissors, cut out the semicircle, cutting through all four layers of paper. Discard the circles cut from the cards.

4. Turn on the flashlight and lay it on a table. Tape the sheet of paper on the wall behind the table so that the light from the flashlight hits the paper. The paper will be the screen.

5. Darken the room and pick up the index cards.

6. Hold the cards so that the cut-out areas overlap, then hold the cards so that the cut-out areas are in front of the light.

7. Keep one of the cards stationary, then slowly slide the other card about ½ inch (1.25 cm) to one side, and return it to its original position. As the cards are moved, notice the size and the brightness of the light spot on the paper screen.

8. Repeat step 7 three or more times.

Results

The size and the brightness of the light on the screen increases, then decreases, as the size of the hole in the overlapping cards increases and decreases.

Why?

Variable stars increase and decrease in size and brightness. This investigation models a **Cepheid variable,** which is a type of variable

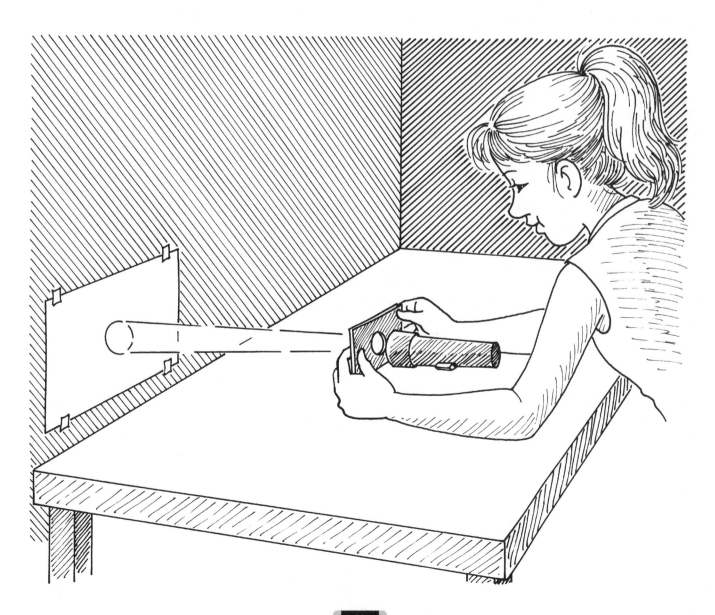

star that changes in brightness, generally in the range of 1 to 50 days. Cepheids change in brightness because their surface layers expand and contract. The increase of the size of the opening in the card represents the expanding surface of a Cepheid, which results in a brighter light. The contracting surface of a Cepheid, which produces a dimmer light, is represented by the smaller hole in the cards.

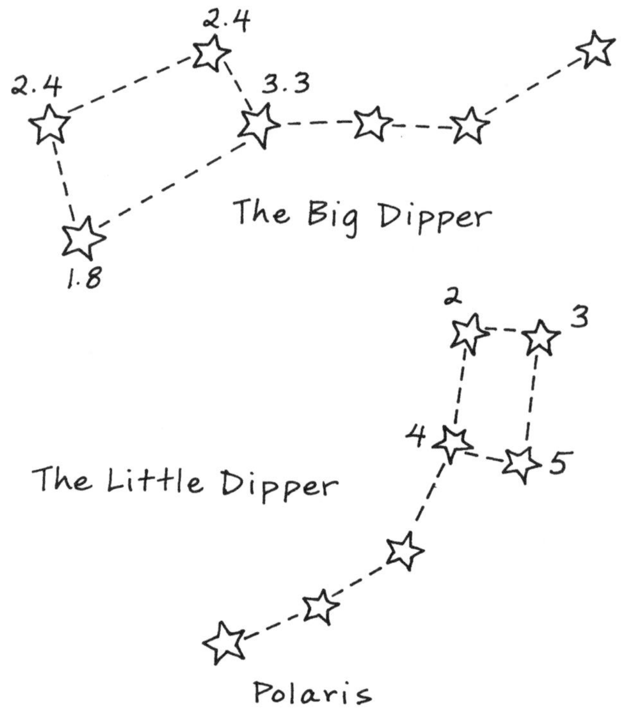

MORE FUN WITH STARS!

Stars vary widely in brightness. Some appear very bright, while others are barely visible to the naked eye. Hipparchus (190–120 B.C.), a Greek astronomer, devised a scale to measure apparent magnitude. He gave a value of 1 to the brightest star and a value of 6 to the dimmest. By 1917, using photographic plates, Leavitt had identified stars near the **North Pole** (the most northern point on Earth and the north end of Earth's axis) with magnitudes from 4 to 21. The stars making up the bowls of the Little Dipper (an asterism in Ursa Minor) and the Big Dipper range in magnitude from 1.8 to 5 (as shown in the diagram). Find these star groups in the northern sky, and compare the brightness of their stars with one another. Look for other stars in the sky, and determine their magnitudes by comparing them with the stars in the dippers.

The Big Dipper

The Little Dipper

Polaris

BOOK LIST

Bernstein, Leonard, Alan Winkler, and Linda Zierdt-Warshaw. *Multicultural Women of Science*. Maywood, N.J.: Peoples Publishing Group, Inc., 1996. Biographical sketches of women of science along with hands-on activities.

Stille, Darlene R. *Extraordinary Women Scientists*. Chicago: Children's Press, 1995. The contributions to science of a few courageous, pioneering women who became scientists.

VanCleave, Janice. *Constellations for Every Kid*. New York: Wiley, 1997. Facts and fun, simple experiments about stars and constellations.

20

Antoni van Leeuwenhoek

Antoni van Leeuwenhoek (1632–1723) was born in Delft, Holland. He attended school as a young child but received no higher education or university degrees and knew no languages other than his native Dutch. He came from a family of tradesmen. His father was a basket maker, while his mother's family were brewers. His father died when Antoni was five.

In 1648, at the age of 16, Leeuwenhoek went to Amsterdam to be an apprentice in a shop

that sold cloth. In 1654, he returned to Delft and married Barbara de Mey, the daughter of a silk merchant. Leeuwenhoek's wife died in 1666, and he was remarried in 1671, to Cornelia Swalmius, who died in 1694. Four of his five children died young, and his surviving daughter, Maria, looked after him until his death.

Leeuwenhoek is believed to have been introduced to a simple microscope in order to count the threads in cloth to determine the cloth's quality. A **simple microscope** (a magnifier with a single lens) is also called a magnifying glass or a magnifying lens. During a visit to London in 1668, he saw magnified pictures of textiles in a copy of Robert Hooke's book *Micrographia*. This book may have started Leeuwenhoek thinking about magnifying things, but there is no evidence of his interest in magnification before 1671. It was in that year that Leeuwenhoek apparently began his journey into the microscopic world.

Even though Leeuwenhoek was not formally trained as a scientist, his detailed descriptions of things that he saw under his microscopes proved to be of great value to science. In 1673, Leeuwenhoek reported his first microscopic observations (bee mouthparts and stingers, a human louse, and a fungus) to the newly formed Royal Society of London (a scientific group that encouraged scientific investigations). He was appointed a member of the Royal Society in 1680 and wrote hundreds of letters to the Society during his lifetime, all in Dutch. (Most scientists were educated and wrote in Latin, which was the accepted common scientific language.)

Leeuwenhoek used simple microscopes, even though the **compound microscope** (a magnifier with a combination of two lenses) was invented in the early 1600s. That's because these early compound microscopes distorted the shape and the color of the specimen under examination. This problem worsened as lenses were made larger and stronger. Leeuwenhoek discovered that simple microscopes made with very small and very **convex** (curved outward like the outside of a ball) lenses provided a clearer **image** (the likeness of an object formed by a lens or a mirror). He made more than 400 simple microscopes that could magnify over 200 times, with clearer, brighter images than the compound microscopes of his day, which generally only magnified up to 50 times. Each microscope consisted of a 3- to 4-inch (12.5- to 20-cm) -long brass plate body with a small hole in which a tiny lens was mounted. Some of the lenses were not much bigger than the head of a pin. The **specimen** (a sample or an object being studied) was mounted on a sharp point that stuck up in front of the lens. Leeuwenhoek kept his method of making lenses and illuminating the specimens a secret.

Leeuwenhoek was also the first person, using a microscope, to observe clearly and to describe red blood cells, as well as sperm (male sex cells), in humans and other animals. Leeuwenhoek incorrectly believed that sperm contained a child in miniature, which grew larger inside the female's body.

Leeuwenhoek is the founder of bacteriology and **protozoology** (the study of **protozoa**—the name for animal-like single-celled organisms). On September 17, 1683, Leeuwenhoek sent the Royal Society a description of what may have been the first observation of bacteria. At least, it was the first recorded observation. He found what is now believed to be bacteria in the scrapings from his own teeth and from those of an old man who claimed never to have cleaned his teeth. He called the tiny moving creatures he saw "animalcules." He devised a counter that allowed him to count the numbers of creatures in a very small sample and then calculate numbers in a larger volume. It is not surprising that the most animalcules were found in the scrapings from the old man's teeth.

Leeuwenhoek had limited knowledge of the scientific discoveries of other scientists, since they reported their findings in Latin and he spoke only Dutch. But because of his curious nature and his interest in lenses, Leeuwenhoek made some of the most important discoveries in the history of biology. He studied anything that he could get in front of the lens of his microscope, including pepper. He wanted to see if it had spikes that might cause the hot, painful taste when eaten. (It is now known that chemicals in pepper cause its burning taste.) Once he almost lost his eyesight observing a small explosion of gunpowder.

Leeuwenhoek described himself as a person who had a greater craving for knowledge than did most other men. He felt it was his duty to record his findings so that others would be informed about his discoveries. He shared what he saw but not his procedure of making viewing instruments.

During the seventeenth century, lenses were commonly crude. Often glass was simply smashed between pieces of wood, and different broken pieces were used for lenses. In studying the Leeuwenhoek microscopes, scientists have determined that Leeuwenhoek discovered that blown glass bubbles had a thicker section at the bottom. He chipped out this thick part and ground glass into particular shapes to make lenses for his microscopes. He developed a way to grind powerful lenses, but no one has discovered how he did this. Only 9 of the more than 500 microscopes made by Leeuwenhoek exist today.

FUN TIME!

Purpose

To determine how much a simple microscope magnifies.

Material

magnifying lens
graph paper

Procedure

1. Lay the magnifying lens on the graph paper.

2. Move the lens so that as many of the horizontal lines as possible can be seen through the lens. Count and record the number of horizontal lines seen through the lens as L_1.

3. Raise the lens to a height where the lines are enlarged but clearly seen.

4. At this height, repeat step 2. Record the number of lines as L_2.

5. Determine the magnification of the lens, using the following equation:

$$M = L_1 \div L_2$$

For the example figures, $L_1 = 8$, $L_2 = 4$, thus the magnification of the lens is calculated by the following equation:

$$M = L_1 \div L_2$$
$$M = 8 \div 4 = 2$$

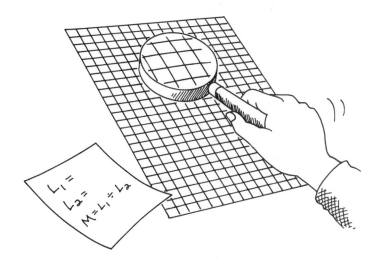

Results

In the example, the magnification of the lens is 2, which means that the graph paper looks twice as large as normal when seen through the simple microscope.

Why?

The lens's shape bends light rays coming from the lines on the paper. Your eyes see the light as though it came in a straight line from the paper, and the image of the squares appears to be enlarged.

MORE FUN WITH LENSES!

Make a simple microscope by cutting a 1-by-6-inch (2.5-cm-by-15-cm) strip from thick cardboard, such as a poster board or the back of a writing tablet. Use a paper hole punch to cut a hole in the center of the paper strip. Fold the ends of the strip as shown and place the strip on a page of newspaper. Position the paper so that light from a window or a lamp shines on it.

First look through the hole at the newspaper, and make note of the size of the printed letters on the paper. Rub cooking oil over the edge of the hole in the strip. Then, place a drop of water on the paper strip near the hole. With your finger, rub the water across the hole. The water should form a thin film across the hole. If not, try again. Dip your finger in water, and let a drop of water fall on the water-covered hole so that a rounded water drop forms in the hole. Look through the water-filled hole at the printed letters. The water forms a convex lens, which curves outward; it has a thick center and thinner edges. Light passing through a convex lens is bent inward, or made to **converge** (the refracting of light rays so that they meet at a spot called the **focal point**). The water-drop lens acts like a magnifying lens, which bends incoming light so that an enlarged, virtual image of the object (the letters) appears beyond it. The image is called **virtual** because it is perceived only by the viewer's brain and cannot be produced on a screen. If the letters look smaller than they do when you are not looking through the lens, you have formed a **concave lens,** which curves inward and reduces the size of the letters. A concave lens is shaped like two dishes placed back-to-back. Light passing through a concave lens bends outward, or **diverges.** When you look through a concave lens, you see a small virtual image.

Add more water to make a convex lens. To focus your microscope (make the letters easier to see by changing the distance of the lens from the letters), move the folded ends of the paper in and out.

BOOK LIST

Haven, Kendall, and Donna Clard. *100 Most Popular Scientists for Young Adults.* Westport, Conn.: Teacher Ideas Press, 1999. Biographies and professional paths of a hundred popular scientists, including Leeuwenhoek.

Headstrom, Birger. *Adventures with Microscopes.* Mineola, N.Y.: Dover Publications, 1977. Microscope projects, as well as a brief history of the microscope.

Levine, Shar. *The Microscope Book.* London: Sterling Publications, 1997. An interesting project book that teaches the basics of microscopy.

VanCleave, Janice. *Microscopes and Magnifying Lenses.* New York: Wiley, 1993. Fun, simple experiments about simple and compound microscopes.

21

Maria Mitchell

America's first acknowledged woman astronomer, Maria Mitchell (1818–1889), was born on Nantucket, a small island off the coast of Massachusetts. She was the third of ten children born to William and Lydia Mitchell. She was taught by her father as a young child and attended a school for young ladies for a while but was largely self-educated.

Mitchell's father, the head of Nantucket's first free school and an amateur astronomer, not only encouraged her to study astronomy but felt strongly that girls should receive an education equal to that of boys. This was an unusual attitude for that time. The emphasis at his school was on observing nature and learning by doing. Students went on field trips to collect specimens, such as flowers and seashells. This shockingly modern method of instructing by observation was later used by Mitchell during her own teaching career.

At 17, Mitchell opened a school for girls. Following in her father's footsteps, she encouraged her students to learn by discovery. Her students often arrived at school early and stayed late for special studies, such as watching birds and studying stars. Her school closed after one year because she accepted a position as a librarian, a job she held for 20 years. It was the perfect job for her, because she loved to read and was able to use the books in the library to further her own education.

Mitchell continued her astronomy studies with her father at an observatory that he built atop the Pacific Bank where he worked. On October 1, 1847, Mitchell looked at the sky through a 2-inch (5-cm) telescope and discovered a new comet. The king of Denmark had offered a medal for the discovery of any new comet, and Mitchell won it, but the award didn't come easily. There were no phones or telegraphs to make her announcement, and on the island, the mail was picked up and delivered only twice a week by boat. Her letter did not leave Nantucket until October 4, and in the meantime, on October 3, two other astronomers, one in England and one in Rome, saw and reported Mitchell's comet. After some discussion, it was determined that Maria Mitchell had been the first to see the comet, and she was awarded the medal for its discovery a year later. The comet was named "Miss Mitchell's Comet."

The Danish medal led to other honors, including her becoming the first woman elected to the American Academy of Arts and Sciences in Boston in 1848. Mitchell remained their only woman member until 1943, when the anthropologist Augusta Fox Bronner (1881–1966) was inducted. Mitchell also became the first woman member of the American Association for the Advancement of Science in 1850.

In 1865, Mitchell's fame led to her becoming the first professor of astronomy and the director of the college observatory at the newly founded Vassar College in Poughkeepsie, New York. Mitchell used the same hands-on method of instructing as before. She refused to issue grades because she didn't think there was a grading unit that could evaluate human minds. She did not require attendance in her class because she believed that if she was a good teacher, students would want to attend. Mitchell was a beloved teacher and **mentor** (a wise and trusted counselor and/or teacher) to a generation of women scientists and is remembered for her ability to motivate. She is quoted as saying, "Did you learn that from a book or did you observe it yourself?" This hands-on approach to instruction is now the most recommended method to teach and encourage students in science studies. Mitchell taught at Vassar until 1888, when she retired due to illness. She died the following year.

Although Mitchell was famous for discovering a comet, her real interest was in the Sun. She worked with her students in the observatory to record changes in **sunspots** (dark spots on the Sun's surface), by making daily photographs over a period of time. In July 1878, Mitchell traveled over 2,000 miles (3,200 km) by train to join other astronomers in witnessing an event that would last exactly 2 minutes and 40 seconds. Mitchell, along with her sister (Mrs. Phebe Kendall) and four Vassar graduates, camped on a hill outside Denver, Colorado, waiting to see the **solar eclipse** (when the Moon blocks the Sun's light) of 1878. This was a bold thing for a group of women to do at that time.

Even with her fame, being a woman scientist was not always easy, so in 1873, Mitchell assisted in founding the American Association for the Advancement of Women, to help other women become educated and pursue careers. She served as the association's president from

1874 to 1876. After her death, her friends and supporters founded the Maria Mitchell Association on Nantucket in 1902. This organization honors America's first woman professor of astronomy and is dedicated to furthering science education, encouraging women in science, and serving as a science resource for Nantucket. In 1994, she was elected to the National Women's Hall of Fame in Seneca Falls, New York.

FUN TIME!

Purpose

To model a solar eclipse.

Materials

golf ball–size piece of modeling clay
2 pens
Styrofoam ball, 4 inches (10 cm) in diameter
flashlight

Procedure

1. Pull off a grape-size piece from the clay piece and mold it into a ball.

2. Stick the clay ball on the pointed end of one of the pens. The clay ball represents the Moon.

3. Stick the point of the other pen into the Styrofoam ball. This ball represents Earth.

4. Use the remaining clay to stand the Earth model on a table.

5. In a darkened room, turn on the flashlight. Hold it in your left hand, about 12 inches (30 cm) from the Earth model.

6. Hold the Moon model in your right hand, in front of the light and about 1 inch (2.5 cm) from the model Earth. Notice the shadow the Moon casts on Earth's surface.

Results

The shadow of the Moon model covers a small area on the surface of the Earth model.

Why?

An **eclipse** is when the light of one celestial body is blocked by another. In this experiment, the Moon eclipses the Sun, which is called a solar eclipse. When the Moon passes directly between the Sun and Earth, the Moon blocks the light from the Sun's **photosphere** (the bright visible surface of the Sun). If the **umbra** (the inner, darker part of a shadow) of the Moon's shadow reaches Earth, to observers in this part of the shadow, the Sun's light is totally blocked, and people experience a **total solar eclipse.** To observers in the **penumbra** (the outer, lighter part of a shadow) of the Moon's shadow, the Sun's light is partially blocked and they experience a **partial solar eclipse.** Observers outside the shadow experience no solar eclipse. Because the Moon orbits Earth and Earth rotates, the Moon's shadow sweeps a narrow path across Earth's surface. Since the average width of the umbra is only about 100 miles (160 km) wide, only a few places on Earth experience a total solar eclipse.

MORE FUN WITH ECLIPSES!

When the Moon is far enough from Earth to appear smaller than the Sun, the Moon does not completely eclipse the Sun. Thus most of the Sun's photosphere is blocked, except for an outer ring. This event is called an **annular eclipse.** Demonstrate an annular eclipse by holding the pen with the Styrofoam ball at arm's length in your left hand so that it is in front of your face. Close your left eye and hold

the pen with the clay ball in front of but not touching your open eye. Slowly move the clay ball away from your face until only a small outer ring of the Styrofoam ball is visible around the clay ball.

BOOK LIST

Colombo, Luann. *Beakman's Book of Dead Guys and Gals of Science.* Kansas City, Mo.: Andrews and McMeel, 1994. The feats and genius of fifteen scientists of the past.

Gormley, Beatrice. *Maria Mitchell: The Soul of an Astronomer.* Grand Rapids, Mich.: Wm. B. Eerdmans, 1995. Mitchell's story, including her efforts to encourage young women in science.

Sammartino, Stephanie. *Rooftop Astronomer: A Story about Maria Mitchell.* Minneapolis: Carolrhoda Books, 1990. A biography of Maria Mitchell, America's first woman astronomer. A story of her struggles and successes as a woman scientist.

Stille, Darlene R. *Extraordinary Women Scientists.* Chicago: Children's Press, 1995. A biography of different women scientists.

VanCleave, Janice. *Astronomy for Every Kid.* New York: Wiley, 1991. Fun facts and investigations about the Sun.

22

Sir Isaac Newton

The English scientist Sir Isaac Newton (1642–1727) was born at Woolsthorpe in Lincolnshire. His father, a wealthy landowner, died shortly before Newton was born. When Newton was three years old, his widowed mother, Hannah, remarried, left Isaac in the care of his grandmother, and went away to live with her new husband. Newton's later writings indicate that he was angry about his mother leaving him, and he disliked his stepfather. As a child, Newton threatened to burn down the house with his mother and his stepfather inside. Although he didn't commit this violent act, his relationship with his mother never was very positive.

Newton was about 11 years old when his stepfather died and his mother returned with two daughters and a son from her second marriage. Although his mother had inherited money and property from both Newton's father and her second husband, some say that she did not share this wealth with Newton, and he went to college as a sizar. A **sizar** was someone who was given an allowance by the college toward college expenses, in exchange for waiting on other students. Other reports indicate that a distant relative was Newton's patron and financed his education. Newton did later return to his mother's home, and she supported him.

Little is known about the details of Newton's early childhood. Some say that he was a loner, and he entertained himself by making complex toys. In one story, Newton is credited with building a working toy windmill that was driven by mice running on a treadmill. Another report claims that Newton caused a UFO scare by flying his kites with lanterns attached. But these stories were written after he was a known scientist and mathematician and just may be what someone thought this genius would have done as a child. It is known that the boy who played alone apparently grew up to be a conceited and difficult man who had many disagreements with other scientists of the day. He was considered odd, made hardly any friends, and was obsessed by his work.

Stories of Newton's education also vary from one account to the next. Some say that the Gratham Grammar School that he attended as a teen provided his early training in mathematics. Others report that after entering college, he purchased an astronomy book and was shocked at his own lack of knowledge of the mathematics it contained. So he taught himself mathematics. Either way, Newton became very knowledgeable in mathematics and science and is credited with having written the single most important book in the history of science. This famous work, published in 1687, is the *Principia Mathematica.* The book contains, among other things, information about gravity, as well as about the three laws that describe the motion of all objects.

Newton's first law of motion defines inertia, which is the property of matter that causes it to resist any change in motion. In other words, an object at rest remains at rest and an object in motion remains in motion unless acted upon by a force.

Newton's second law of motion describes how a force acting on an object causes the object to accelerate. It is a relationship between force, mass, and acceleration. The greater the force on an object, the greater the acceleration. The smaller the mass, the greater the acceleration produced by a certain amount of force. The equation that expresses this law is: $F = m \times a$, which is read: force (F) equals mass (m) times acceleration (a).

Newton's third law of motion is called the law of action and reaction, and it relates the forces that two objects exert on each other. In other words, a reaction might be that object A pushes on object B. The reaction would be that object B pushes back on object A with an equal force but in the opposite direction.

Newton was asked how he made the astonishing discoveries contained in the more than 500 pages of *Principia Mathematica,* and his reply was, basically, that he continuously thought about them. Actually, he had been thinking about the concepts in the book for many years. One particular "thinking period" in his life occurred around 1665, when the bubonic plague—known as the Black Death— struck England. This plague was caused by a bacteria transmitted to humans by flea bites from infected rats. Because of the plague, Newton left college and returned to his mother's farm in Lincolnshire, England. There he spent his time wondering about things in nature, such as "Is the force that causes apples to fall the same force that keeps the Moon in orbit around Earth?" He concluded that it was. Of course, the famous story about Newton is that he discovered gravity when an apple fell on his head. All we know for sure is that there were apple trees on his mother's farm.

Newton did not spend all of his time sitting around thinking. He also experimented, including unwisely experimenting on himself by putting objects underneath his eyeball. He wanted to determine what would happen when pressure was applied to the eye. His notes indicate that after one such experiment, he had to lie in bed for two weeks with the curtains drawn. He could have blinded himself and in fact may have damaged his eyes.

Newton was also fascinated by light. He used a prism to experimentally show that white light is made up of different colors. But his published reports about light were not accepted by all scientists of the day. The English scientist Robert Hooke (1635–1703) claimed that Newton's ideas were either not correct or not original or that Hooke had done it all before. After hearing the criticism of his theories on light, Newton retreated into his shell and said he would not publish anything. Newton waited twenty years, until after Hooke had died, to publish his work on light, entitled *Opticks,* in 1704.

In 1669, Newton became a professor of mathematics at Cambridge. From 1669 to 1687 was Newton's most productive period, in which he did his mathematical research and writings. Then around 1687, Newton became a highly paid government official in London and seemed to have little interest in mathematical research. From that time until his death in 1727, he began to perform strange experiments that had to do with alchemy (a mixture of science and magic that dealt with changing less-expensive metals into gold and with finding ways to prolong life indefinitely). He had several periods of severe depression, and some think that his depression may have been the result of his being poisoned by some of the chemicals in his experiments.

FUN TIME!

Purpose

To demonstrate Newton's first law of motion.

Materials

marker
two 3-ounce (90-mL) paper cups
pencil
two 24-inch (30-cm) pieces of string
transparent tape
10 pennies
1 drinking straw

Procedure

1. Use the marker to label the cups "A" and "B."

2. Use the pencil to punch 2 holes beneath the rim and on either side of each cup.

3. Thread 1 string through the holes in each cup and tie the ends of the strings to form a loop.

4. Using the tape, secure the ends of each string loop to the edge of a table. Adjust the strings so that the cups hang an equal distance below the table's edge.

5. Place the coins in cup "B."

6. Sit on the floor in front of cup "A." With the end of the straw about 6 inches (15 cm) from cup "A," blow the smallest puff of air toward the cup to start the cup swinging. Make a mental note of the effort that's necessary to supply the air needed to move the cup.

7. Repeat step 6, using cup "B."

8. Compare the effort needed to supply the air to move the 2 cups.

Results

It took more effort to supply the air needed to move cup "B" than to move cup "A."

Why?

Newton's first law of motion states that every object stays at rest or in motion unless it is acted on by outside forces. This is also called the law of inertia. In this experiment, at first the cups were not moving, which means they were at rest. You supplied an outside force on each cup, your exhaled breath, causing the cups to accelerate (change from an at-rest velocity of zero to a velocity greater than zero). Cup "B" had more mass than cup "A." Since you had to blow harder to move cup "B," your experiment agrees with Newton's second law of motion, that the more massive an object is, the greater is its inertia, thus the greater the outside force needed to accelerate it. Because cup "B" is more massive than cup "A," it has more inertia, so it takes a greater outside force to accelerate it.

MORE FUN WITH INERTIA!

A magician's trick of pulling a tablecloth out from under a table setting and leaving the dishes standing can be explained by inertia. You can do a simplified version by knocking a paper loop from beneath a coin. Do this using a 1-by-24-inch (1.25-by-600-cm) strip of poster board. Secure the ends of the paper with tape to form a loop. Set the loop on a quart (1 liter) jar. Balance a penny on top of the loop directly above the center of the jar's mouth. Sweep the end of the pencil past one side of the loop and strike the inside of the opposite side so that the pencil carries the loop away and the coin drops in the jar. You may need to practice a few times before performing this trick for friends.

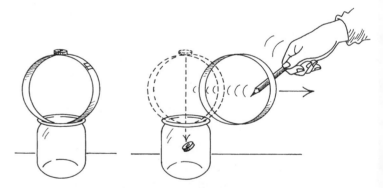

BOOK LIST

Cements, Gillian. *The Picture History of Great Inventors.* New York: Knopf, 1994. Focuses on major inventors and scientists, such as Newton, and includes a time line giving a glimpse of other events that took place during that era.

Parker, Steve. *Isaac Newton and Gravity.* Broomall, Pa.: Chelsea House, 1995. A biography of Newton, including his accomplishments and life experiences.

Reid, Struan, and Patricia Fara. *The Usborne Book of Scientists.* New York: Scholastic, 1992. A book about the lives and the work of some of the world's greatest scientists, including Newton.

VanCleave, Janice. *Physics for Every Kid.* New York: Wiley, 1991. Fun, simple science experiments, including information about inertia.

23

Louis Pasteur

The French chemist Louis Pasteur (1822–1895) was born in Dole, France, but grew up in the nearby city of Arbois. Louis was one of three children, and the only son, of Jeanne and Jean-Joseph Pasteur. His father was a **tanner** (a person who changes the hides of animals into leather), and even though his family was poor, his parents wanted Louis to have a good education. Louis married Marie Laurent in 1849, and they had five children: four girls and a boy.

In elementary school, Louis was considered a shy, stupid boy who was more interested in fishing and drawing than in schoolwork. He may have been shy, but he was far from stupid. He spent hours painting and had his two sisters pose for him for such long periods that their necks and backs ached. He worked hard at what he wanted to do and insisted that others work as hard as he did. He could have become a great artist, but his father did not want him to do this professionally because it was difficult for most artists to make a living. Louis's father wanted him to teach at a nearby college.

Pasteur did so well as a student at college that he was encouraged to apply to the École Normale, a French university in Paris, founded specifically to train outstanding students to become university science and writing teachers. Pasteur was accepted and started school but became so homesick that he left after his first year. He returned a year later, and it was then that he became interested in chemistry. In 1847, he earned a doctorate degree from the École Normale, with a focus on both physics and chemistry. He took a job as an assistant to one of his teachers and started his memorable science career by studying the shapes of **crystals** (solid materials in which the atoms or the molecules are arranged in repeating patterns).

Pasteur discovered that some crystals are made of **molecules** (particles made of two or more atoms) that are exactly alike except that they are mirror images of each other, just as your hands are mirror images of each other. Since mirror-image molecules can be thought of as being left-handed and right-handed, they are called **chiral molecules,** from the Greek word for "hand."

Pasteur studied different crystals, including those found in the sediment that naturally separates from wine during fermentation. He discovered that during fermentation, the left-handed crystals were not affected by microbes. This discovery led Pasteur to study fermentation as both a chemical and a biological process, instead of just a chemical process, which was the accepted idea of the day. It was thought that the microbes called yeast promoted fermentation when they died and decayed. Pasteur's work showed that fermentation depended on living microbes and that each microbe fed on specific foods. It was later discovered that living microbes promote fermentation by releasing chemicals called **ferments** (enzymes that cause the fermentation of foods).

Further investigations of fermentation led to Pasteur's discovery that while yeast promotes the formation of alcohol, the presence of a certain bacteria causes the alcohol to change to an acid called vinegar. He discovered that heating killed the bacteria and suggested that wine be heated before storing it to kill any bacteria in it. This process of heating foods, such as wine and milk, to kill bacteria is called pasteurization, after Pasteur.

In 1683, Leeuwenhoek first reported the presence of bacteria in material observed through his homemade microscopes. But until Pasteur, no one had made the connection between bacteria and diseases. In 1865, Pasteur published what was known as his "germ theory of disease," which claimed that most infectious diseases were caused by microbes called germs.

In 1885, Pasteur treated Joseph Meister, a nine-year-old boy who had been repeatedly bitten by a rabid dog. **Rabies** is a deadly infection caused by a specific microbe that usually enters the body through the bite of an animal. Pasteur had successfully cured dogs that had been infected with the rabies germ by injecting them with a weak solution of rabies germs. The parents of the boy knew the child would die without help, so they brought him from Alsace, Germany, to Paris and begged Pasteur to try the treatment on their son. It worked, and Pasteur's treatment for rabies became his greatest triumph. He received gifts of money that allowed him to build his own private research laboratory, the Pasteur Institute, where he remained the director until his death. Pasteur solved the mysteries of rabies, anthrax, chicken pox, cholera, and silkworm diseases and contributed to the development of the first vaccines, but, tragically, he was unable to help three of his daughters who died of typhoid fever.

Pasteur won many awards for his work, but some of his ideas were not widely accepted, for example, his belief that many patients died after surgery due to infections caused by germs on dirty instruments and surgeons having dirty hands. One elderly surgeon was so angry over this accusation that surgeons were harming their patients that he challenged Pasteur to a duel. Pasteur did not accept the challenge. He was not likely to be dueling with anyone because in 1868, at age 46, he had a **stroke** (damage to the brain due to the lack of blood flow). The stroke caused paralysis of his left side. But some supported his theory of trying to decrease bacteria by cleanliness. One of his supporters was Joseph Lister (1827–1912), an English surgeon who used clean surgery techniques and discovered antiseptics, which led to a decrease in infected wounds. Today not only do health-care workers wash their hands often, but special instruments are used to heat surgery instruments in order to kill the germs on them.

FUN TIME!

Purpose

To model Pasteur's left-handed and right-handed molecules.

Materials

pencil
4-inch (10-cm) square piece of white copy paper
poster paint: any color

Procedure

1. Use the pencil to write "Left" along one edge of the paper and "Right" along the opposite edge.

2. Fold the square of paper in half by placing the left and the right sides together.

3. Unfold the paper partway and place 2 pea-size blobs of paint about ½ inch (1.25 cm) apart in the center of the fold.

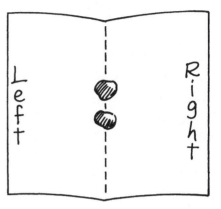

4. Fold the paper, and use your fingers to spread the paint by pressing and rubbing the paper in two directions as shown.

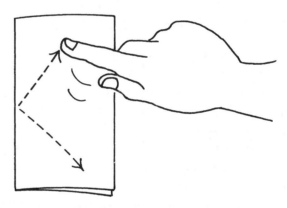

5. Unfold the paper and allow it to dry. Observe the shape of the paint designs on both sides of the fold.

Results

The size and the shape of the paint design on the left and the right sides of the fold are mirror images of each other.

Why?

Pressing the paper together forces the paint to spread out. When the paper is unfolded, the paint separates, leaving mirror-image prints. The print on the left is called the left-handed print and the one on the right is the right-handed print. When the paper is folded along a center line, the prints fit perfectly together.

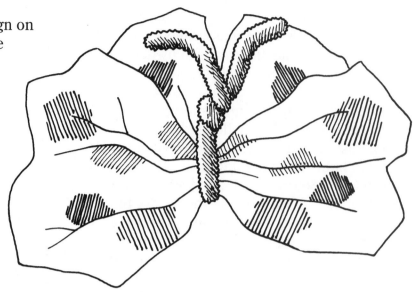

MORE FUN WITH MIRROR-IMAGES!

Mirror images are found in other parts of nature, such as butterfly wings. The shapes and colors of the wings on the left side of a butterfly's body are mirror images of the shapes and colors on its right side. Make a butterfly model to show mirror-image wing patterns. Do this by folding a round coffee filter in half. Place a piece of newspaper on a table to protect the table. Unfold the filter and lay it on the newspaper. Randomly place 6 to 8 pea-size blobs of different colors of paint on the filter. Fold the filter in half along the center fold line and press the paper together. Unfold the filter and allow it to dry. Squeeze the filter

together down the fold, and twist a 6-inch (15-cm) piece of black pipe cleaner around the filter to form the body and the antenna of the butterfly, as shown.

BOOK LIST

De Kryuif, Paul. *Microbe Hunters.* New York: Harcourt, Brace and Company, 1996. The human side of the earliest researchers into microbes, including Pasteur.

Meadows, Jack. *The Great Scientists.* New York: Oxford University Press, 1997. The biographies of twelve great scientists, including Louis Pasteur.

VanCleave, Janice. *Food and Nutrition for Every Kid.* New York: Wiley, 1999. Fun facts and investigations about fermentation and other food topics.

World Book Looks at Inventions and Discoveries. Chicago: World Book, Inc., 1996. How some of the world's great inventions and discoveries were made, including those by Pasteur, and how they affected people's lives.

24

Sir Benjamin Thompson
(Count Rumford)

Sir Benjamin Thompson (1753–1814)—later known as Count Rumford—was born in Woburn, Massachusetts. At the age of 18 he went off to Rumford, Massachusetts, where he soon married a wealthy widow fourteen years his senior. It is said that because of her influence, he became a major in the colonial **militia** (a military force made up of part-time citizen-soldiers who were trained to serve in times of emergency). He later applied to serve in George Washington's Continental Army during the Revolutionary War but was rejected, apparently because his fellow officers from the militia found him so disagreeable. It seems that he really remained loyal to the English. When it was discovered that he was a British spy, he left his wife and his child and fled to England.

In England, he devoted himself to making friends with people who could help him become successful. Eventually, he had a high-ranking position in the Bavarian army. (Bavaria is now a state in southeastern Germany.) For eleven years he served in the administrative offices of the Bavarian civil and military service. In recognition of his service to Bavaria, he was knighted in 1784 and in 1791 he was made a count of the **Holy Roman Empire** (a region of land in central and western Europe). He began to call himself Count Rumford, after the town of Rumford in America. Although no one knows why he wanted to use this name, it's Count Rumford that history remembers.

Rumford investigated heat and made many practical heat-related inventions, including central heating for buildings, a fireplace with a special design that conserved heat and produced less smoke, the pressure cooker, a drip coffee-pot, and, most useful to those in the military, thermal underwear. But his main contribution to science was his explanation of what heat is and what it is not. In 1798, while supervising the **boring** (drilling a hole through a material) of metal cannons for the Bavarian army, he noticed that heat was produced during the process. This experiment caused him to disagree with the currently accepted **caloric theory of heat** proposed by the chemist Antoine Lavoisier. This theory described hot objects as having more caloric than colder objects had. Caloric was believed to be an invisible, weightless substance that flows from a hot object to a cold object when they were in contact. Rumford experimentally proved that this theory was incorrect. He correctly hypothesized that the cannons did not contain caloric. Instead, it was the motion of boring and what we now called **friction** (a force that opposes the motion of two surfaces in contact with each other) that caused the cannons to become hot. At first, Rumford's ideas were not accepted, and some say that it was because of his abrasive personality. But soon others repeated his experiments and agreed with his ideas that friction produces heat.

It is ironic that Rumford married Marie-Anne Lavoisier, the widow of the beheaded scientist whose heat theories Rumford discredited. This marriage lasted only a short time. Count Rumford lived his later years in England and France, absorbed in his scientific studies and in writing scientific papers. He died in Auteuil, near Paris, at the age of 61.

FUN TIME!

Purpose

To show that friction can cause materials to heat up.

Materials

pencil with eraser
index card

Procedure

1. Touch the index card with your fingers, and note how hot or cold the card feels.

2. Press the eraser of the pencil against the card.

3. Quickly move the eraser back and forth across the card, as you slowly count to 10.

4. Repeat step 1. Compare the temperatures of the card before and after rubbing it with the eraser.

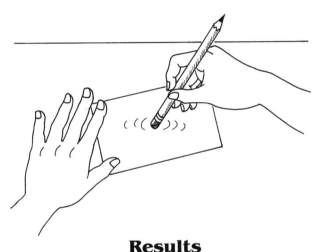

Results

The card is hotter after you rub it with the eraser.

Why?

Friction is the name of forces that oppose the motion of two surfaces that are in contact with each other. Using the friction between the eraser and the card, you converted **mechanical energy** (the energy of an object that is moving or has the potential of moving) into thermal energy. When you touched the rubbed card, it felt hot because heat from the card was transferred to your skin.

MORE FUN WITH FRICTION!

Friction causes things that rub together to wear down, as well as to heat up. A **lubricant** (a substance that reduces the friction between two surfaces that move against each other) is used between the moving parts of machines to help reduce friction. You can see the effect of a lubricant by first pressing the palms of your hands together, then quickly rubbing your hands back and forth as you count to 10. Note how warm your hands feel. Repeat the procedure after spreading a small amount of hand lotion over the palm of one hand.

BOOK LIST

Brown, G. I. *Scientist, Soldier, Statesman, Spy: Count Rumford: The Extraordinary Life of a Scientific Genius.* Gloucestershire, U.K.: Sutton Publishing, 2000. A historical account of Count Rumford's achievements and escapades.

Orton, Vrest, and Austin Stevens. *Observations on the Forgotten Art of Building a Good Fireplace.* Chambersburg, Pa.: Alan C. Hood & Co., 2000. A biography of Sir Benjamin Thompson, better known as Count Rumford.

VanCleave, Janice. *Physics for Every Kid.* New York: Wiley, 1991. Fun, simple physics experiments, including information about friction, heat, and energy.

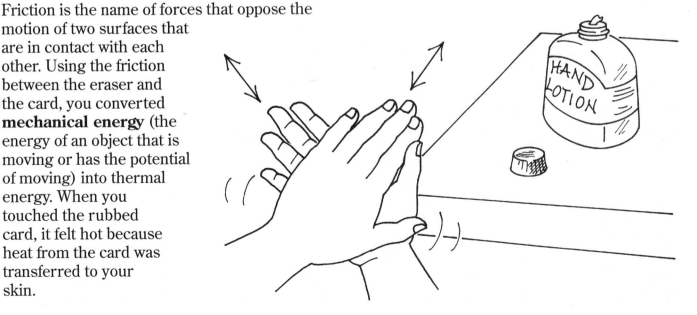

25

Rosalyn Sussman Yalow

In 1974, the American medical physicist Rosalyn Sussman Yalow (1921–) became the first American-born woman to win the Albert Lasker Basic Medical Research Award, which is one of the highest science awards in the United States. In 1977, she became the second woman to receive the Nobel Prize in medicine and the first American woman to receive such an honor. None of this surprised her family, who know her to be a very determined person. Rosalyn describes herself as having been a stubborn child who, once she had decided to do something, could not be stopped from achieving her goal.

Rosalyn's mother, Clara Zipper Sussman, came to the United States from Germany at the age of four. Her father, Simon Sussman, was born in New York. Neither of her parents had a high school education, but they were well-read. Rosalyn could read before she was in kindergarten. Rosalyn's parents never doubted that their two children, Alexander and Rosalyn, would graduate from college. In 1941, Rosalyn graduated with honors in physics and chemistry from Hunter College in New York.

Yalow wanted to continue with her education, but it was very unlikely that a good graduate school would accept and offer financial support for a woman in physics. However, because the United States was about to enter World War II, many men who would have been in graduate school were in the military. So in 1941, Yalow became a teaching assistant in physics at the University of Illinois, and it was from this university that she earned her Ph.D. in nuclear physics in 1945. During her time at the University of Illinois, she met and married A. Aaron Yalow, a fellow physics student.

Yalow taught physics from 1946 to 1950 at Hunter College. In 1950, she began a long-lasting partnership with Dr. Solomon A. Berson, a physician. Berson and Yalow worked together at the Bronx Veterans Administration Hospital, researching the use of radioisotopes in medicine. **Radioisotopes** are radioactive forms of chemical elements. Yalow and Berson used radioisotopes as **biochemical locators,** which meant that the radioisotopes were used to "tag" chemicals in the body, such as insulin. When radioactive insulin was injected into a body, the movement of the tagged insulin in the body could be traced with radiation-detecting instruments. The movement of the tagged insulin helps physicians to identify problems inside the body. Berson died before the work was completed. Although the loss of her coworker and friend of twenty-two years was devastating, Yalow continued her endeavors and in 1977 won the Nobel Prize in medicine for her work with radioisotopes.

While being a scientist was one of Yalow's goals, being a wife and a mother was also part of her plan. She believes that women can successfully balance a career and family life. Yalow encourages women to pursue science careers and to believe in themselves, or no one else

will. She is known for saying that the world cannot afford the loss of the talents of half its people if it is to solve its many problems. Yalow retired from the VA hospital in 1991. She is using her time and her prestige as a Nobel Prize winner to encourage science education and to promote other causes.

FUN TIME!

Purpose

To model biochemical locators.

Material

pencil
one 12-inch (30-cm) square piece of poster board
disk magnet
transparent tape
scissors
10-inch (25-cm) pipe cleaner (found at craft stores)
ruler

Procedure

1. Use the pencil to draw the shape of a body on the poster board.

2. Place the magnet on a table and lay the poster board on the table so that the body diagram is over the magnet. Tape the poster board to the table.

3. Using the scissors, cut the pipe cleaner into 20 or more small pieces.

4. Spread the pipe cleaner pieces across one end of the poster board.

5. Hold the ruler on its edge and move the pipe cleaner pieces across the poster board until some of the pieces stand up. The standing pipe cleaners mark the spot above the magnet.

magnet under poster board

different shapes and sizes of magnets, such as bar magnets, solid disks, and disks with holes through their centers. Place the magnets under a piece of poster board, and use pipe cleaners of different colors to form colored patterns. Once the patterns are formed, you may wish to remove the pipe cleaners one at a time, dip the end of each pipe cleaner in glue, and replace it on the poster board. When the glue dries, a three-dimensional image is produced. A colored pen could also be used to add parts to the pattern, such as the stem and the leaves for the flower pattern shown.

Results

As the pipe cleaners move across the paper, the ones above the magnet stand at an angle to the paper.

Why?

Because the pipe cleaners are made of steel, they will cling to the magnet and can be used to locate the magnet beneath the paper. The pipe cleaners represent radiation-detecting equipment, and the magnet represents the biochemical locators—radioisotopes. Radioisotopes give off radiation, which is a type of energy that can be located by a special radiation-detecting camera. A special image is shown from the points that emit radiation. This image can be magnified by a computer and displayed on a monitor so that a physician can look for indications of problems.

MORE FUN WITH LOCATORS!

Different types of radioisotopes and their amounts in the body produce different images. A fun way to model these differences is to use

BOOK LIST

Bernstein, Leonard. *Multicultural Women of Science.* Maywood, N.J.: Peoples Publishing Group, 1996. Biographical sketches of notable women of science, including Rosalyn Yalow, with a hands-on activity for each scientist.

Stille, Darlene. *Extraordinary Women Scientists.* Chicago: Childrens Press, 1995. Biographies of women scientists, including Rosalyn Yalow.

Straus, Eugene. *Rosalyn Yalow, Nobel Laureate: Her Life and Work in Medicine.* New York: Perseus, 2000. A biography of Rosalyn Yalow.

Red Cabbage Indicator

Materials

red cabbage
knife
cutting board
1-cup (250-mL) measuring cup
electric blender
4 cups (1000 mL) distilled water
large strainer
large bowl
tape
marking pen
refrigerator

Procedure

1. Cut enough red cabbage into small pieces to fill the cup.

2. Pour the cabbage pieces into the blender. Then add 4 cups (1000 mL) of distilled water.

3. Blend the water and the cabbage.

4. Hold the strainer over the bowl and empty the contents of the blender into the strainer.

5. Pour the cabbage juice from the bowl into the jar and discard the solid pieces of cabbage left in the strainer.

6. Use the tape and marking pen to label the jar "Red Cabbage Indicator."

7. To prevent spoilage, store the indicator in a refrigerator until needed. It should be discarded after seven days.

Scientist Timeline

A timeline of the scientists mentioned in this book, listed in order of birthdates.

625?–?546 B.C.	Thales
c.460–c.370 B.C.	Democritus
450–370 B.C.	Leucippus
384–322 B.C.	Aristotle
c.372–c.287 B.C.	Theophrastus
287–212 B.C.	Archimedes
190–120 B.C.	Hipparchus
c.100–c.170	Claudius Ptolemy
965–1039	Alhazen
1452–1519	Leonardo da Vinci
1473–1543	Nicolaus Copernicus
1544–1603	William Gilbert
1546–1601	Tycho Brahe
1564–1642	Galileo Galilei
1571–1630	Johannes Kepler
1602–1686	Otto von Guericke
1622–1703	Vincenzo Viviani
1623–1662	Blaise Pascal
1627–1691	Robert Boyle
1629–1695	Christiaan Huygens
1632–1723	Antoni van Leeuwenhoek
1635–1682	Johann Becher
1635–1703	Robert Hooke
1642–1727	Sir Isaac Newton
1660–1734	Georg Stahl
1686–1736	Gabriel Daniel Fahrenheit
1701–1744	Anders Celsius
1706–1790	Benjamin Franklin
1728–1779	James Cook
1733–1804	Joseph Priestley
1738–1822	William Herschel
1740–1799	Horace de Saussure
1743–1794	Antoine-Laurent Lavoisier
1744–1829	Jean-Baptiste de Lamarck
1745–1827	Alessandro Volta
1747–1826	Johann Elert Bode
1750–1848	Caroline Herschel
1753–1814	Sir Benjamin Thompson (Count Rumford)
1766–1844	John Dalton
1769–1823	Edward Jenner
1769–1859	Alexander von Humboldt
1772–1864	Luke Howard
1774–1857	Francis Beaufort

1778–1829	Sir Humphry Davy
1790–1852	Gideon Mantell
1791–1872	Samuel Morse
1797–1875	Charles Lyell
1799–1847	Mary Anning
1806–1873	Matthew Maury
1809–1882	Charles Darwin
1818–1889	James Prescott Joule
1818–1889	Maria Mitchell
1822–1884	Gregor Johann Mendel
1822–1895	Louis Pasteur
1827–1912	Joseph Lister
1833–1896	Alfred Bernhard Nobel
1847–1922	Alexander Graham Bell
1847–1931	Thomas Alva Edison
1852–1908	Antoine-Henri Becquerel
1852–1911	Jacobus H. van't Hoff
1859–1906	Pierre Curie
1859–1927	Svante August Arrhenius
1859–1953	Alice Eastwood
1863–1941	Annie Jump Cannon
1867–1934	Marie Curie
1868–1921	Henrietta Leavitt
1870–1938	Ynes Mexia
1871–1937	Ernest Rutherford
1879–1955	Albert Einstein
1880–1930	Alfred Wegener
1881–1955	Alexander Fleming
1881–1966	Augusta Fox Bronner
1897–1956	Irène Joliot-Curie
1898–1968	Howard Walter Florey
1902–1922	Barbara McClintock
1906–1979	Ernst Boris Chain
1907–1964	Rachel Carson
1910–1994	Dorothy Crowfoot Hodgkin
1916–	Francis Crick
1920–1958	Rosalind Franklin
1921–	Rosalyn Sussman Yalow
1926–	Paul Berg
1928–	James Watson
1934–	Jane Goodall
1942–	Steven Hawking

Glossary

abiotic   Nonliving things.

acceleration   The change in the velocity of an object.

acid   An aqueous solution containing hydronium ions—H_3O^{+1}. A substance that has opposite characteristics of a base. A substance that makes a red cabbage indicator turn from purple to red.

air   The name given to the mixture of gases in Earth's atmosphere.

alchemist   A scientist who practices alchemy.

alchemy   A mixture of science and magic that dealt with changing less-expensive metals into gold and with finding ways to prolong life indefinitely.

altitude   The height of an object above Earth's surface, or above sea level.

Alvin   A manned submersible.

amber   Fossilized tree sap.

anemometer   An instrument used to measure wind speed.

annular eclipse   When only an outer ring of the Sun's photosphere is visible to observers during a solar eclipse.

antibacterial   Destructive to the growth of bacteria.

antibodies   Chemicals in the body that help protect the body from a disease caused by a specific organism.

antiseptic   A substance that kills or prevents the growth of germs on body surfaces.

apparent magnitude   A measure of how bright a star appears.

aqueous solution   A mixture in which one or more substances are dissolved in water.

arc   Portion of a circle.

artificial satellite   Any object purposely placed into orbit around Earth, other planets, or the Sun; man-made satellites.

asterism   A group of stars with a shape within a constellation.

astrology   A study that assumes that the positions and motions of celestial bodies, particularly the Sun, the Moon, the planets, and the stars at the time of a person's birth affect the person's character, and therefore his or her destiny; a pseudoscience.

astronomer   A scientist who studies celestial bodies.

astronomy   The study of all the celestial bodies in the universe.

atmosphere   The blanket of gases surrounding a celestial body.

atmospheric pressure   The force that gases in the atmosphere exert on a particular area.

atom   The building block of all materials.

attract   To pull together.

axis   The imaginary line through the center of an object.

bacteria   A type of microorganism. Some are useful and some cause diseases.

bacteriology   The study of microorganisms.

barometer   An instrument used to measure atmospheric pressure.

base   An aqueous solution containing hydroxide ions—OH^{-1}. A substance that has opposite characteristics of an acid. A substance that makes a red cabbage indicator turn from purple to green.

battery   A device that changes chemical energy into electrical energy.

bellows   A device whose sides are squeezed to pump out air.

biochemical locators   Radioisotopes used to tag chemicals in the body so that the chemicals' movements can be traced.

biochemicals   Substances found in living organisms.

biochemist   A scientist who studies things dealing with living organisms and the chemical reactions of life processes.

biochemistry   The study of the substances found in living organisms and of the chemical reactions of life processes.

biographical   About a person's life.

biologist   A scientist who studies organisms.

biology   The study of different organisms.

biotic   Living things.

black hole   Thought to be an extremely dense celestial body that has such strong gravity that not even light can escape from it, therefore, it appears black.

boring The act of drilling a hole through a material.

botany The branch of biology dealing with the study of plants.

botanist A scientist who studies plants.

braille A system of writing for blind people using raised dots for letters that are "read" with one's fingertips.

buoyancy The upward force of a fluid on an object placed in it. The ability to float.

caliph A Muslim ruler.

caloric An invisible, unweighable substance inside materials that was believed to flow from a hot object to a cold object when the two objects were in contact.

caloric theory of heat A theory proposed by the chemist Antoine Lavoisier, describing hot objects as having more caloric than colder objects have.

camera obscura A device that produces the temporary image of an object.

carbon An element found in organic chemicals; a black substance called soot that is left when things burn.

catalase An enzyme found in almost all cells.

celestial bodies The natural objects in the sky, including suns, moons, planets, and stars.

cells The building blocks of organisms.

Cepheid variable A type of variable star that generally changes in brightness in the range of 1 to 50 days.

chain reaction A nuclear reaction in which some of the products of the reaction cause the reaction to keep going.

charging by induction A process of charging a neutral material by holding a charged object near but not touching it.

chemical Any substance with a definite composition made up of one or more elements.

chemical reaction A process by which atoms interact to form one or more new substances.

chemist A person who studies chemistry.

chemistry The study of the makeup and the structure of chemicals, as well as of how they change and combine.

chiral molecules Mirror-image molecules that are left-handed and right-handed.

chromosome A rod-shaped structure in cells that is made up of genes.

cloning The process of producing an organism from one cell of a single parent.

closed circuit An unbroken circuit.

combustion The process of rapid combination with oxygen or the burning of a substance.

comet A small celestial body made up of dust, gases, and ices (mainly, water and carbon dioxide) that moves in an extremely elongated orbit around the Sun.

compound microscope A magnifier with a combination of two lenses.

concave lens A lens that curves inward like the surface of a plate. Light passing through a concave lens is refracted outward, or made to diverge.

condense A change from a gas to a liquid.

constellation A group of stars that forms a pattern.

convection currents The movement of water due to differences in temperature.

converge In reference to light, it is rays of light refracting so that they meet at a spot called the focal point.

convex Curved outward like the outside of a ball.

convex lens A lens that curves outward; it has a thick center and thinner edges. Light passing through a convex lens is refracted inward, or made to converge.

cosmology The branch of astronomy dealing with the study of the universe as a whole, including its distant past and its future.

cosmologist A scientist who specializes in cosmology.

crescent phase The lighted part of the Moon that looks like a ring segment with pointed ends.

crystal A solid material in which the atoms or molecules are arranged in repeating patterns.

decay 1. The spontaneous change of the nucleus of a radioactive element into another. 2. The breakdown of plant and animal materials by natural means.

decomposition Breaking into smaller parts.

density The measure of the amount of matter in a known volume of a material.

dinosaur An extinct land-dwelling reptile.

dirt The common name for soil.

displaced To take the place of something.

diverge In reference to light, it is rays of light bending outward so that they do not meet.

dominant Refers to the stronger of a pair of traits. When present, the dominant trait determines the trait of the offspring.

double stars Two stars that appear to be close together.

earth science The study of Earth from the outermost limits of its atmosphere to the innermost depths of its interior.

eclipse When the light of one celestial body is blocked by another.

ecologist A scientist who studies living things and their environments.

ecology The study of the relationship between plants and animals and their environments.

electrical charge The property of particles within atoms that causes the particles to attract or repel one another or other materials.

electrical insulator A material that does not easily allow electricity to flow through it.

electric current A flow of electric charges.

electricity A form of energy associated with the presence and the movement of electrical charges.

electric circuit The path of an electric current.

electric discharge The loss of static electricity.

electric lamp A device that gives off light; commonly called an electric lightbulb.

electrons Negative particles spinning around the nucleus of an atom.

elements The basic chemical substances of which all things are made; substances that contain only one kind of atom and that cannot be broken down into simpler substances.

elliptical The shape of a slightly flattened circle.

elocution The art of speaking clearly.

emission The release of something.

energy The capacity to move matter from one place to another; the ability to do work.

enzyme A chemical found in organisms that changes the speed of chemical reactions in the organism.

environment All the external factors affecting an organism, including abiotic and biotic factors.

equator The imaginary line around the center of Earth.

era A period of time in history.

eroded To be broken apart and moved away.

extinct No longer in existence.

fermentation A chemical reaction in which microbes growing in the absence of air cause changes in food.

ferments Enzymes that cause the fermentation of foods.

filament The fine thread that gets hot and gives off light in a lamp.

fluid A gas or a liquid.

focal point A spot where converging light rays meet.

force A push or a pull on an object.

forecasting Predicting a future event.

fossilist A person who is very knowledgeable about fossils.

fossils The remains or traces of prehistoric plants and animals.

friction A force that opposes the motion of two surfaces in contact with each other.

genes The units of heredity described by Mendel.

genetic engineering The application of the knowledge obtained from genetic investigations.

geneticist A scientist who studies things dealing with heredity.

genetics The branch of biology dealing with the study of heredity.

geocentric Earth-centered.

geologist A scientist who studies things dealing with the composition of Earth and its history.

geology The study of the composition of Earth and its history.

germs A term used by Pasteur to describe microbes that cause infectious diseases.

gravitational acceleration The change in the speed of an object due to the force of gravity; 32 ft/sec^2 (9.8 m/sec^2).

gravity A force of attraction between all objects in the universe; a force pulling objects toward the center of Earth; a force equal to the weight of an object, usually measured in newtons or pounds.

heat The energy transferred from one body to the other, due to differences in temperature.

heliocentric Sun-centered.

heredity The transfer of traits from parents to offspring.

heresy An act against the teachings of a church, especially by a person professing the beliefs of that church.

Holy Roman Empire A region of land in central and western Europe.

humidity The measure of the amount of water in air.

humus The material formed by decomposed organisms.

hydrographer A scientist who measures, describes, and maps Earth's surface waters.

hydronium ion The ion found in aqueous acid solutions; H_3O^{+1}.

hydroxide ion The ion found in aqueous base solutions; OH^-.

hydroxyl A product of the reaction between hydrogen peroxide and superoxide that kills bacteria.

hygrometer An instrument used to measure humidity.

hypothesis A guess, based on facts, about the answer to a question.

image The likeness of an object formed by a lens or a mirror.

incandescence The emission of light due to the high temperature of an object.

incandescent Glowing due to incandescence.

inertia The property of matter that causes it to resist any change in motion.

inverted   Upside down.

ion   An atom or group of atoms that has lost or gained one or more electrons.

law of conservation of matter   A law stating that the quantity of matter involved in a chemical reaction does not change.

lens   A piece of glass or other transparent material so shaped that it refracts light passing through it.

leukemia   Cancer of the blood.

lubricant   A slippery substance that is placed between two moving surfaces to reduce friction.

luminesce   To give off light.

lysozyme   An antiseptic found in some body fluids, such as tears.

mass   The measure of the amount of matter in an object; it is commonly measured in metric units of grams or kilograms.

matter   The substance from which all objects are made; anything that takes up space and has mass.

mechanical energy   The energy of an object that is moving or has the potential of moving.

mentor   A wise and trusted counselor and/or teacher.

meteorologist   A person who specializes in meteorology.

meteorology   The study of Earth's atmosphere and especially the study of weather.

microbes   Tiny organisms visible only under a microscope, such as bacteria; also called microorganisms.

microbiologist   A scientist who studies microscopic organisms, including the prevention of diseases caused by them.

microbiology   The study of microbes.

militia   A military force made up of part-time citizen-soldiers who were trained to serve in times of emergency.

minor planet   An asteroid.

molecule   A particle made of two or more atoms.

Moon phases   The regularly recurring changes in the shape of the lighted part of the Moon, facing Earth.

mythology   The study of myths of a particular culture.

myths   Stories that express the beliefs of a group of people or deal with basic questions about the nature of the world.

natural satellite   A celestial body that orbits a larger celestial body; planets are natural satellites of the Sun.

naturalist   A person who studies plants and/or animals.

neutron   An uncharged particle inside an atom's nucleus.

Newton's first law of motion   The scientific principle that states that every object stays at rest or in motion unless it is acted on by outside forces.

Newton's second law of motion   The scientific principle that describes how a force acting on an object causes the object to accelerate.

Newton's third law of motion   The scientific principle called the law of action and reaction that relates the forces that two objects exert on each other.

North Pole   The most northern point on Earth and the north end of Earth's axis.

Northern Hemisphere   The region north of the equator.

nuclear energy   Energy releases as a result of splitting or fusing atomic nuclei.

nuclear fission   The splitting of a large nucleus into two smaller nuclei.

nuclear physics   The study of the nucleus of an atom.

nuclear reaction   The change of the nucleus of an atom.

nucleus   The central part of an atom.

ocean convection currents   The movement of water in a circular pattern, as a result of lighter, warm, less dense water rising, while heavier, cool, more dense water sinks.

oceanography   The study of oceans, including the organisms in them.

oceanographer   A scientist who specializes in oceanography.

offspring   The young of a particular organism.

open circuit   A circuit with a break in it so that no current can flow.

optical double stars   Two stars that appear to be close to each other but are actually far apart and have no true relationship.

optics   From the Greek word *optikes,* originally meant the study of the eye and of vision; the study of all phenomena related to light.

orbit   The curved path of one object around another.

organic chemicals   Substances containing the element carbon; found in organisms.

organisms   Living things.

paleontologist   A scientific observer of fossils.

paleontology   The study of prehistoric animal and plant life through the careful examination of fossil remains.

parallel circuit   A circuit in which the electric current divides and follows two or more paths.

partial solar eclipse   On Earth, it occurs in areas where the penumbra of the Moon's shadow reaches Earth's surface.

particle radiation Particles given off from the nucleus of some elements.

pasteurization The process of heating foods, such as wine and milk, to kill bacteria.

patron A person who supports another, providing a salary and living expenses.

penumbra The outer, lighter part of a shadow.

pesticide A chemical used to kill unwanted organisms, such as insects.

phase change A change in which one phase of matter changes to another.

phases of matter The three common forms of matter: solid, liquid, and gas.

phenomena (singular—**phenomenon**) Observable events.

philosopher A person who searches for knowledge for its own sake.

philosophy The study of truth, wisdom, and knowledge.

phologiston An invisible, weightless substance in materials that can burn.

phologiston theory A description of burning as the result of the presence of phlogiston.

photometer An instrument that changes light from a distant star into an electric current.

photon A packet of energy that has both wave and particle properties.

photosphere The bright visible surface of the Sun.

physicist A scientist who studies the properties and relationships of energy and matter and the laws of motion.

physics The study of the properties and relationships of energy and matter and the laws of motion.

principle A basic truth, law, rule, or belief.

prism A triangular-shaped piece of transparent material that refracts the rays of white light passing through it so that the light separates into different colors, called the spectrum.

product A substance that is produced in a chemical reaction.

prolific Productive.

proteins Chemicals in the body that are used in almost everything cells do.

proton A positive particle in the nucleus of an atom.

protozoa A name for animal-like, single-celled organisms.

protozoology The study of protozoa.

pseudoscience A set of beliefs pretending to be scientific but not based on scientific principles.

rabies A deadly infection caused by a specific microbe that is not carried by matter.

radiation Energy that can move through space and that is not carried by matter.

radioactive A term coined by Marie Currie to describe the ability of an element to spontaneously give off what is now known as particle radiation.

radioactive element An element in which the nucleus breaks apart, giving off particles and energy.

radioactivity The spontaneous emission of energy as a result of changes in the nucleus of an atom.

radioisotope A radioactive form of a chemical element.

reactant A substance that is changed during a chemical reaction.

recessive Refers to the weaker of a pair of traits; doesn't determine the trait of an offspring if a dominant unit is present.

reflecting telescope A telescope that uses mirrors and lenses to gather the light from a distant object and enlarge the image of the object.

refraction The change of the direction of a wave as it moves from one medium to another; in reference to light, it is the bending of light as it moves from one transparent material to another.

relative motion The description of motion from a specific frame of reference.

repel To push apart.

revolve To move in an orbit around an object.

rotate To turn on an axis.

scientist A person who observes and/or experiments to discover answers to scientific questions.

SCUBA Self-Contained Underwater Breathing Apparatus; a portable breathing device for divers.

sea level The level of ocean water.

sediment Rock, sand, or dirt, that has been carried to a place by water, wind, or ice. Solid particles that settle to the bottom of a liquid.

semisynthetic penicillin A synthetic penicillin, which is a mixture of natural mold and synthetic materials.

series circuit A circuit with only one path for the electric current.

simple microscope A magnifier with a single lens.

sizar A student given an allowance by the college toward college expenses, in exchange for waiting on other students.

soil The top layer of Earth's surface that supports plant life. It is composed of particles from rock mixed with humus.

solar eclipse When the Moon eclipses the Sun.

solution A mixture of a substance that has been dissolved in a liquid.

soot Carbon; a black substance left when most things burn.

specimen A sample or an object being studied.

spectrum A band of colors, in the order red, yellow, orange, green, blue, indigo, and violet, produced by separating white light.

spontaneous Happening by itself.

static charges The buildup of stationary electrical charges.

static electricity Any effect due to static charges.

stroke Damage to the brain due to a lack of blood flow.

submerged Sunken or pushed beneath the surface of a fluid.

submersible A sea craft that can function underwater at great depths.

sunspots The dark spots on the Sun's surface.

switch A device that is used to close and open a circuit.

synthesized Man-made.

synthetic Man-made, not natural.

tanner A person who changes hides of animals into leather.

telegraph A device used to send and receive a code of electrical signals.

telephone An instrument that changes sound into electrical messages and back again.

telescope An instrument that permits distant objects to be viewed as if they were brighter and closer to the observer.

temperature How hot or cold something is.

terminator The boundary between the light and the dark sides of the Moon.

terrestrial Land.

theory An idea or a statement that explains how or why something happens, based on all known evidence but can be changed as new information is discovered.

theory of continental drift An idea that the continents were once connected but over time drifted apart.

theory of natural selection A theory based on the fact that all living organisms compete for water, food, shelter, and so on, for survival.

thermal energy The internal energy that affects the temperature of an object.

thermometer An instrument used to measure temperature.

total solar eclipse On Earth, it occurs in areas where the umbra of the Moon's shadow reaches the Earth's surface.

traits Characteristics.

transparent A characteristic of an object that allows light to pass through it.

tuberculosis A lung disease.

tungsten A metal that has the highest melting point of all metals.

twilight The small amount of light at daybreak or at sundown.

umbra The inner, darker part of a shadow.

universe All the celestial bodies throughout space, including Earth, regarded as a whole.

vaccine A substance containing dead, weakened, or living microorganisms that can be injected into the body or taken orally in order to cause the body to produce antibodies against a particular disease.

variable stars Stars that change greatly in brightness over a period of time, some changing in only hours or days, and others requiring years.

velocity The speed in a particular direction of an object.

vibrate To rapidly move up and down or back and forth.

virtual image An image that is perceived only by the viewer's brain and cannot be produced on a screen, such as the image seen when viewing an object through a magnifying lens.

vocal physiology The study of how the body produces sound.

volume The amount of space taken up by an object.

weather The condition of the atmosphere at a certain time and place.

white blood cells The part of blood that fights germs.

work The amount of force on an object times the distance the object moves in the direction of the force.

zoology The branch of biology dealing with the study of animals.

zoologist A scientist who studies animals.

Index